In the Key of

NEW YORK CITY

In the Key of
NEW YORK CITY

A Memoir in Essays

Rebecca McClanahan

🐓 Red Hen Press | *Pasadena, CA*

Book design by Mark E. Cull

Library of Congress Cataloging-in-Publication Data

Names: McClanahan, Rebecca, author.
Title: In the key of New York City : a memoir in essays / Rebecca McClanahan.
Description: First edition. | Pasadena, CA : Red Hen Press, [2020]
Identifiers: LCCN 2019048868 (print) | LCCN 2019048869 (ebook) | ISBN 9781597098502 (trade paperback) | ISBN 9781597098519 (ebook) Subjects: LCSH: McClanahan, Rebecca. | Authors, American—20th Century—Biography. | New York (N.Y.)—Biography. | New York (N.Y.)—Anecdotes.
Classification: LCC PS3554.E9274 A6 2020   (print) | LCC PS3554.E9274 (ebook) | DDC 818/.5409 [B]—dc23
LC record available at https://lccn.loc.gov/2019048868

The National Endowment for the Arts, the Los Angeles County Arts Commission, the Ahmanson Foundation, the Dwight Stuart Youth Fund, the Max Factor Family Foundation, the Pasadena Tournament of Roses Foundation, the Pasadena Arts & Culture Commission and the City of Pasadena Cultural Affairs Division, the City of Los Angeles Department of Cultural Affairs, the Audrey & Sydney Irmas Charitable Foundation, the Kinder Morgan Foundation, the Meta & George Rosenberg Foundation, the Allergan Foundation, the Riordan Foundation, Amazon Literary Partnership, and the Mara W. Breech Foundation partially support Red Hen Press.

First Edition
Published by Red Hen Press
www.redhen.org

Acknowledgments

"Signs and Wonders," first published in *River Teeth*, was a notable listing in the *Best American Essays 2004* and reprinted in *Short Takes: Brief Encounters with Contemporary Nonfiction* and in the *River Teeth Reader*. "The Music in the Walls," which appeared in *Literal Latte* as "The New Couple in 5A," was a notable listing in the *Best American Essays 2018*. A longer version of "Book Marks" appeared in the *Southern Review* and was reprinted in the *Best American Essays 2001* and the *Best American Essays Fourth College Edition*. "'And We Shall Be Changed': September 7–11, 2001" appeared in the *Kenyon Review*. "Shirley, Goodness, and Mercy" (originally titled "Back") appeared in the *Gettysburg Review* and received Special Mention in the *Pushcart Prize 2007*. "Adopt a Bench," first published in the *Sun*, was listed as notable in the *Best American Essays 2015* and received Special Mention in the *Pushcart Prize 2015*. Portions of "Sublet" and "Su–Thrivingly" appeared in the *Bellingham Review*. Portions of "Present Tense" (originally titled "Nest") appeared in *Shenandoah*. "Tears, Silence, Song" was published in the *Kenyon Review*. A longer version of "Ginkgo Song," which appeared in the *Kenyon Review*, was listed as notable in the *Best American Essays 2013*. "Our Towns" appeared in the *Gettysburg Review*. "Early Morning, Downtown 1 Train" appeared, in slightly different form, in the *Georgia Review*.

Thanks to long-loved friends who read these pages and offered valuable criticism: Fleda Brown, Barbara Conrad, Jessica Handler, Gail Peck, Diana Pinckney, Barbara Presnell, Lia Purpura, Mike Steinberg, and Dede Wilson. Thanks also to those who cheered from the sidelines, especially Martha Allen, Anna Duke Reach, Mimi Schwartz, Eunice Tiptree, Nancy Zafris, and my always expanding family tribe.

During the New York years, Elise Handelman and Bob Nathanson supplied laughter when I needed it, Karen and Richard Ruta opened their beautiful home to us, and Amy and Rob Roy cooked dinners, poured wine, and shared their amazing daughters. My gratitude extends to the New York acquaintances who became friends, especially Janice Eidus, Kim Dana Kupperman, Mindy Lewis, Joan Lonergan, Madge McKeithen, John Merrow, Tish Romer, Dustin Beall Smith, Carol Sterling, and Anna Stoessinger.

My students and colleagues at Hudson Valley Writers Center, *Kenyon Review* Writers Workshop, Queens University MFA, and Rainier Writing Workshop provided warm and accepting forums for early versions of this book.

I am indebted to the editors who have supported my work, especially Robert Atwan, Stephen Corey, Mark Drew, Geeta Kothari, Dan Lehman, David Lynn, Joe Mackall, Dinty W. Moore, R.T. Smith, and Peter Stitt. And I extend deep gratitude to Peggy Shumaker, most generous human being, who championed this manuscript and introduced me to Red Hen Press, whose amazing editor, Kate Gale, supported by other members of the Red Hen family, guided me every step of the way.

Most importantly, I am grateful beyond measure to Donald Devet, my husband and inspiration, who shared the New York journey and continues to sustain me with humor, warmth, insight, and patience. No one could wish for a better partner.

Contents

Author Note

Life interrupts the memoir. The memoir interrupts the life. More than twenty years have passed since my husband and I made our midlife move to New York City. We'd expected to stay for perhaps two years; we stayed for eleven, and our departure was as sudden and uncalculated as our arrival had been, due in part to increasing family responsibilities. New York has changed greatly since our time there, as have our personal lives. My father, who is alive on the pages of the memoir, died in 2016, and my mother, whose presence animates many of the book's events, has entered the advanced stages of dementia. Nephews and nieces who appear in the book as teenagers now have children of their own. And, as if to complete the journey my husband and I began, shortly after we moved back to North Carolina, two of my nieces moved to New York to begin their own adventures in the city that we once called our own. Life moves in strange and marvelous patterns; the memoir runs panting behind the life but can never catch up. This book is an attempt to hold, in this moment, a time and place that changed my life in ways I have yet to fully understand.

Signs and Wonders

ARTILLERY SOUNDS WAKE ME: car alarms screeching, beeping—you know the drill—and a jackhammer breaking open the sidewalk outside our window. No, not our window, I remind myself. The window of the apartment we've been subletting this past year, and the lease is almost up. Another year? My husband is leaving it up to me. Donald could live anywhere; he's that kind of guy. Easy, adaptable, like the ducks in the park. Things roll right off his back.

When we first moved to New York, we couldn't believe how cheap the flowers were. "What a city," we said. "We can buy flowers every week, fill the apartment with them, the bathtub. What a city!" Then we went to the grocery store, and when I saw the prices I started to cry. "How can we possibly afford . . . we'll have to give up . . . oh my God," I shrieked, "what will we eat?"

"We'll just have to eat flowers," Donald said.

Last week, I would have signed a hundred-year lease. I was just coming off one of my New York highs, the kind that hits when you least expect it and suddenly it's like first love again, first lust, and you wonder how you could possibly live anywhere else. Then a steam pipe bursts, the couple in the apartment above you straps their steel-heeled boots back on, you step in a puddle of urine on the subway platform, and some guy with three rings in his nose calls you "bitch" and spits on you because—who knows?—you look like his second grade teacher, or some president's wife, or his mother, and you think, Live another year in this jackhammering, siren-screaming, piss-puddling city? In someone else's apartment, in someone else's bed? With someone else's plates, forks, spoons?

Maybe it's the wrong day to decide. Maybe I need some air. Maybe I need a sign. So I go where I always go when I need a sign—to Central Park, and oh look, a day so beautiful you'd gladly pay if the universe were charging. The leaves on the ginkgos are falling, gold coins upon gold coins. And there in the pond are my ducks, how I admire them. Look, one is passing up breadcrumbs to catch a blossom. He's eating flowers.

Along the promenade are the inline skaters in their T-shirts: *Kickimus Maximus Assimus. Are you talking to me? Fun loving criminal.* One guy is skating backward, a small compact man so graceful he doesn't need skates—his hip joints are on ball bearings, rolling in one smooth movement. But I know it's harder than it looks. Isn't everything? If you peek beneath the surface of the water, you can see the ducks' tiny paddle-wheel feet working, churning. It breaks your heart: little New York ducks have to keep moving all the time.

I stop at a bench beside a raggedy guy in a black hat, his shopping cart plastered with handmade signs. New York is a city of signs: *Curb your dog. Curb your dogma. Love your neighbor, your neighbor's dog.* His signs are bright red, painted on cardboard: *Society of Jesus Christ. Society of Disabled Artists. Call me Ray.*

"So, Ray," I say, "you're an artist?"

He rummages in his cart and pulls out a painting of a bonfire, flames breaking into bloom.

"Have you ever seen a flame like that?" I ask. "Or is it imagination?"

"I like to think about Moses," he says. "I was seeing the burning bush."

"God spoke to him in the fire, right?"

"That's right."

"In words?" I ask.

"*Through* him. Spirit."

I tell him I used to be in a gospel choir, but I was only a lowly backup singer.

"Never call yourself lowly," he says.

Closer now, I can see the face beneath the hat: almost handsome. But the smell is ripe, and I won't be staying. Besides, it's his bench; I'm just subletting. A lowly subletter, I think for an instant, then stop myself. But it *is* his bench and I should respect that. I don't like it when people come to *my* gazebo. It took me months to find it, the most beautiful place in the park. There's even a place to fish. I can lean my back against the wooden slats, put my feet up, watch the geese forming their predictable V pattern. It's good to have something to count on, like the gondola that glides through about this time of day, sliding under the Bow Bridge, the gondolier always singing badly "O Sole Mio," which seems a crazy choice for New York: o sole *mio*, oh *my* sun, *my* ducks, *my* forks, oh *my* anything. When so much of New York is about we: *o sole wio*.

Still, it's a beautiful spot, my gazebo, and I'd tell you where it is, but what if word got out? A few weeks ago—on my birthday, no less—I couldn't even get a seat. It hadn't been a good week; the odometer of my life was clicking too fast. Birthdays can do that to you, especially in the city. Especially when you do what we did—wait until middle age to move here. "Like, isn't that backwards?" one of my nieces had said. "I mean, like, don't most people go to New York when they're young?"

So I really needed my gazebo that day, but some guy was stretched out the whole length of it, beside a grocery cart with a handmade sign sticking out of the top: *I'm at the peak of my life.* I wondered if the sign was meant for me, if it was trying to tell me something. A few more clicks on life's meter, and I'll be one of those ancient women sharing a park bench with another ancient woman, the two of us leaning together over a bag of peanuts.

Oh, the partners we make, the families we create in this city of strangers. Like that big guy on Ninth Avenue—big as a truck, I know you've seen him, riding that little bike with the basket on the front. Inside the basket is one of those Cabbage Patch dolls that were popular a decade or so ago. The doll is always dressed for the weather, secured with a homemade seat belt and a miniature helmet. Such care. And yesterday, beside the carousel, I saw a teenage boy strapped into a wheelchair, his head lolling, brown eyes rolling up to the sky, his mouth opening, like a bird's, for a spoon lifted by a large, dark woman. The two were facing each other— he in his wheelchair, she on the green bench. Their knees were touching. Steam was rising from the thermos of soup. First she dipped the spoon in the thermos, then put it to her mouth and tested to be sure the soup was safe, that it wouldn't burn him.

When I see things like that, I want to break into lullaby. Sing someone to sleep in this town that never sleeps. Adopt an artist, a duck, the whole Cabbage Patch family. Look,

REBECCA McClanahan § 15

there's a family now, spilling out of my gazebo, with their fishing poles, their buckets and bait, their beautiful children—black eyes, black hair, dimpled hands—the kind of children you want to touch but you can't, of course, especially in New York. The little boy is wrestling a bright red carp the color of the fire in Ray's painting, and now his sister is catching the carp in a net. Don't they know it's against the rules posted all over the park? *Catch and release.* Look but don't touch. Enjoy for the moment, then let it go—the fiery carp, the brilliant day, the black-eyed children with the dimpled hands, the coins on the ginkgo trees swirling down, down. Our lives are sublets anyway, and too quickly gone at that. And what better place to live out our leases. Curb your dog, your dogma, love your neighbor, your neighbor's dog. We're at the peak of our lives. *O Sole Wio.* Catch and release.

Sublet

THE FIRST TIME I encountered the word, my brain misread it as *subtle*. I was eleven or twelve at the time and, as I recall, I saw the word in some plastic-covered library book, an English novel about cottages and peasants; then, as now, I read whatever I could get my hands on. Wait a minute, I thought, backing up a sentence or two when I realized that what I was reading made no sense: that word wasn't *subtle*. I can't remember if I went to the dictionary my mother kept beside the typewriter or if I just kept reading, figuring that all would become clear sooner or later. Sublet: some kind of weapon, maybe, or one of those long gloves soldiers wore back then, like a gauntlet?

Had I been a New York adolescent, I would not have paused over the word; even in the early 1960s, sublets were common in Manhattan. As for me, living in a suburb twenty miles from Quantico, Virginia, in our fourth or fifth military "post," as our Marine Corps father called the bases where we were stationed every few years, New York might as well have been a foreign country. I'd never known anyone who came from New York. Of course I knew that's where they kept the Statue of Liberty and the Empire State Building, which as a young child I'd misheard as the *Entire State Building*. And I knew that New York was where Lucy and

Ethel lived side by side, and Margie Albright from *My Little Margie*, and where Rob Petrie worked while Laura stayed home somewhere in the suburbs. But that was television, make-believe. As was *West Side Story*, which I'd recently seen at the movie theater, unaware that the production had first been staged on Broadway. Broadway? Oh, yes, I would have remembered, that's near Macy's, where the parade happened in *Miracle on 34th Street*, right?

Unlike Donald, whose family had roots in the city and who visited once or twice a year during his childhood, I'd never dreamed of one day living in New York. I'd never dreamed of New York at all. Had someone told me that I would one day live a few blocks from where the Jets and Sharks rumbled in alleys and Maria lingered hopefully on fire escapes, I would have told them to get their head examined. And had they told me that I would not only live there but that I would be a subletter, I would have had to slink back to that page in my plastic-covered library book, or to the dictionary beside my mother's typewriter, to understand what in the world I was getting myself into.

❧

Fast-forward to 1999, a dark winter morning in Midtown Manhattan. Granted, every morning feels dark from our furnished fifth-floor sublet, where the lone bedroom window, partly obstructed by a bulky window air conditioner, faces a brick wall. Lying in our landlords' platform bed, the covers pulled high around my neck, I hear over the clank and bang of radiators the lascivious cooing of the pigeons that roost, and sometimes mate, on the air conditioner. Some New Yorkers call them flying rats and do whatever they can to discourage their roosting—spikes, netting. I'm not that jaded yet. *Jade* is a strange word, depending on how you turn it in the light. *Jade*: deep green mineral, known for its ability to take an elegant polish; the harder you rub it, the more it shines. *Jade*: a dull, exhausted, ill-tempered horse, ridden too hard and too long, worn out, used up.

Donald is in the kitchen. I hear the squeak of the faucet and the bump of ancient water pipes struggling with their first task of the day. Now he's grinding coffee beans in our grinder, one of the few possessions we brought with us from North Carolina. Now the carafe of the coffee maker is filling.

I slide deeper beneath the covers. Since childhood, I've always been a morning person. "Bright-eyed and bushy-tailed," my night-owl siblings and friends used to say. "Perky." And later, when adolescence claimed us: "Too goddamn perky." What can I say? I loved morning. Maybe I still do. But morning in Manhattan feels different. Darker. Shadowed with, what, exactly? I can't put my finger on it. Exhaustion but not exhaustion, a buzz of excitement and high adrenaline, like a hive of bees humming deep inside my bones. What is their message? What are they humming? *Home*?

But we *are* home, aren't we? That's what we both decided when we sold our house and left our jobs and friends and family and garden and cat: home would be wherever *we* are, together—our bodies, our lives. And haven't things worked out even better than we'd imagined? A part-time teaching position for me, two seminars a week. Several job interviews for Donald, though nothing has panned out yet. No new friends yet either, but lots of out-of-town visitors, family mostly, who ooh and aah over the apartment. "You definitely lucked out," they say.

It's true, we did. We'd done our homework, months before our planned move, contacting everyone we knew who might know anyone in the city with an affordable apartment to lease. We hadn't planned on a furnished sublet; we'd wanted our own things. But you take what you can get. And we got a lot: three rooms of furniture, wineglasses and lamps, brooms and mops, a platform bed complete with sheets and duvet, its under-the-bed drawers filled with the landlords' out-of-season clothes, and a wall of photographs showing an attractive, well-dressed, fortyish man and woman.

"Who are they?" my teenage nephew asked when he came for a visit, bunking near the bicycle that hangs upside down from a giant hook in the ceiling; they'd left the bicycle, too.

"Our landlords," I said.

"That's weird," he said. "To hang pictures of yourself in someone else's place."

He obviously didn't understand. "It's their place," I answered. "We're just borrowing it for a while."

Now behind the bathroom wall, water is roaring into the tub. Then the soft thump, the diverter knob lifting, and the rushing shush of the shower. Absent the light I'd once counted on—the sunlight that spilled through our North Carolina home—what I have come to count on, in this winter of darkness, is water. Water, filtering drip by drip into the carafe of the coffee maker. Water, miraculously converting to steam from a huge boiler in the basement, then snaking up, up, through five stories of hidden pipes, to emerge as heat that hisses through a radiator beside our borrowed bed. Water, filling the prewar cast-iron tub, its porcelain glaze marred and chipped. The deep-as-a-coffin tub I lie down in each evening, turning the faucets to their highest power so that Donald can't hear what might ambush me at any moment.

"Are you still homesick?" my sister asked a few weeks ago when she called from California.

I answered no, which was technically true. Homesick is what I felt when I went to my first sleepaway camp or when the moving van arrived at our next "post" just days before the start of a new school year. Homesick was a soft-focus, bittersweet longing that came in waves, yes, but they were surface, breeze-blown waves that appeared in my periphery, rippled quietly past me, and then gradually subsided. These waves are nothing like that. They come when I least expect them: first a tightening in my throat, then the heated sting behind my eyelids, then the pressure in my chest. Not again, I think. Not now. Thank God for the water gushing from taps, its oceanic roar drowning out the sobs. Shoulder-heaving, childlike sobs.

But that was last night. This is morning. Donald appears in the semi-darkness, dressed for another day of job hunting. I don't know how he keeps up his spirits, week after week, month after month. "Something will turn up," he always says. "Any day now."

He holds a coffee mug out to me. Ah, the Eden of coffee, the first sip.

"Light?" he says, moving toward the reading lamp beside the bed.

"Not yet," I answer groggily. "In a while." My voice sounds low, raspy, Brenda Vaccaro in *Midnight Cowboy* husky but without the sex appeal. Perky is definitely dead.

"Try to have a good day," he says, as if having a good day requires effort. This makes no sense. After all, this is a free morning—no classes to teach, no student manuscripts to read. The day stretches before me, spotless as an unopened ream of paper. There's the promise of coffee, of a new poem or essay waiting at my desk. Or a shopping cart adventure to the overpriced green market, a jog in the park, a few moments on a back pew at St. Thomas listening to the boys' choir rehearse. Our first year here, I used to tour open houses, but it was disheartening to see that the places we might one day afford weren't places where we could imagine ourselves living.

Besides, it saddens me to be in someone's apartment when they aren't there. I start wondering why they're leaving, where they will go next, and if their new place will feel like home. In one Harlem brownstone, which looked as if it had been emptied in a hurry, I saw a drawing on the wall of a tiny, dark bedroom, a crayoned replica of a clothes rack with attached hooks. Above each hook, in a child's loopy printing, was a label: "belts" above one hook, "purses" above another, "necklaces" above another. It stopped my breath. Some little girl's plan, it seemed, had never had time to materialize.

Donald leans down to kiss me goodbye, smelling straight-from-the-shower fresh, his crisply starched shirt collar stiff against my cheek.

"Good luck with the interview," I say.

"I have a good feeling about this one," he says. He pulls back the curtain and raises the Venetian blind. The pigeon couple is there, their beaks locked together. Have we caught them in pre- or post-coital collusion? Blink your eyes and you could miss the show: the bowing and turning, his courtly pirouette, her playing-hard-to-get, back-turned brush-off, the puffing up of his feathers, the unsteady climb onto her back, a quick clap of his wings, then another clap—one, two, applause all around. He bows, she blinks, looks away shyly, tucks her head down.

If you look closely, in just the right light, New York pigeons are beautiful, resplendent in their rainbow oil-spilled hues, the jewel colors of their backs—turquoise, emerald, topaz, jade—reflecting the variations of the sky. As we watch, an updraft from the alley below ruffles her feathers. The wings flutter, revealing delicate white tips. She blinks, he blinks. The warbling starts up again, from deep in the engines of their throats, the cooing, the hum: *home*. Home to roost. Our beautiful sublet pigeons.

The Music in the Walls

EVERY AFTERNOON AT FOUR o'clock, while Donald is still at work, I give up on my writing, set aside my student manuscripts, and wait. Soon, behind the wall that divides our apartment from Apartment 5B, the music begins. First the click of his front door lock. Then the heavy door creaks open and quietly closes; he is not a slammer like most of our neighbors. Then I hear the rattle and ching of keys landing in a bowl. A silver bowl, I imagine, given his classical music training. Two soft thumps (his shoes dropped on the rug?) and the shuffle of feet across the floor. Eight steps, nine.

I place my ear against the wall: the squeak of a hinge as the piano cover opens, a brief hesitation, a few tentative plinks on the keyboard, and then his voice. No lyrics yet. For now only the vowels, the deepest oh's and ah's as he ascends the scale, descends, ascends, closing the space between us.

The first time I heard the singing, neither Donald nor I had met our neighbor in 5B. The owner of the voice, I imagined, was a massive creature, bearded and hulking, with one of those huge, inflatable chests opera stars possess. Perhaps even more impressive than Pavarotti's, for this was no tenor whose bright notes soared to the highest register; this was a bass-baritone with a capital B, his lungs loaded with tones so resonant that their power must have vibrated the floor-boards beneath his feet.

A few days after I heard the singing, as I was returning from an appointment shortly before four o'clock, I saw a young man walking toward 5B. A slight, compact Asian man carrying a grocery bag from D'Agostino, a delivery for the singer, I assumed. The man reached into his pocket and pulled out a key, expertly fitting it into the lock. Click. The heavy door opened, then quietly closed. The keys landed in the bowl. By the time I'd entered our apartment, the music had begun.

Thus began my education in the school of New York apartment dwelling: the first introduction to your neighbors will probably not be a face-to-face meeting but rather a series of sensory clues. In the city we left in North Carolina, the first glimpse of a neighbor was exactly that—a glimpse, in the form of a wave from a front porch or a chance encounter as we swept the sidewalk outside our garden gate. Here in New York, you can live for days, even months, possibly years, without connecting the bodies you pass in the lobby to the aromas filling the hallways—the scent of fresh-baked bread from 5D, for instance, or the pungent sting of curry and turmeric from 5F—or to the sounds you hear through shared walls.

Or through the prewar plaster ceiling, a bedroom ceiling whose light fixture, at about two o'clock in the morning, might begin to shimmy side to side, then pick up speed, perhaps loosening flakes of plaster that drift down onto the bed you share with your husband, who can sleep through anything, as all people must learn to do if they are to live sanely in New York. But when we were new to the city, I had not yet acquired this ability. So every few nights, I would wake at the first thump above our bed, waiting for the light fixture dance to begin and gain momentum, faster now, faster, its rhythm so predictable that I could count down—from twenty, as I recall—until the fixture began to slow, slow, and finally settle.

The first night the ceiling dance began, I waited for the sounds typical of such encounters. The squeak of bed springs. The labored huffs as the twin engines of breath gained momentum. The climactic sighs or cries, followed by post-coital giggles, perhaps, or the sleepy murmurings of long-bedded partners. Instead, there was only the tidal rhythm of, what? Water? A waterbed? Do they allow waterbeds in Manhattan apartments? A waterbed, above our heads?

That was many months ago. If there is indeed a waterbed in the apartment above ours, so be it. I confess that this phrase—*so be it*—is one I've never actually spoken aloud, but I'm trying to practice thinking it, in hopes of entering a state of acceptance about the daily and nightly occurrences that are out of my control. Which is to say, nearly everything. And if I've not yet entered Billy Joel's "New York State of Mind," I am at least accustomed to the rhythmic slosh of the couple in 6A as well as the other cuts on their soundtrack: the stomp of boots across the hardwood floor, a muffled tap-tapping I've yet to identify, the flush of the ancient toilet two or three times a night, and the roar of water that accompanies, I surmise, his morning showers and her evening baths.

Not that I can say for certain that the 6A tenants are a he-and-she, or even that the two constitute a couple. Maybe I just want to believe this. Maybe I've conjured their lives in my mind, the way, based solely on the cigarette smoke that seeps up through the cracked floor molding beside my desk,

I've conjured a lean, leather-jacketed painter in 4A, working round the clock on a huge abstract canvas splattered with violent primary colors. Since I've not yet met the neighbors in 4A and 6A, I am free to imagine.

So, I imagine. And until I meet my neighbors, I will hold to my imaginings. That the painter will soon finish the canvas and invite Donald and me to his next gallery reception, where we will mingle with other art lovers. That the couple in 6A is a fiftyish couple, like us. Wedded amicably and affectionately—thus the dancing light fixture. That, like us, they have cocktails each evening at five thirty, then proceed to their small kitchen to begin preparations for dinner. That, once seated at their dining table, they toast with a decent red wine their good fortune. Then one of them (the wife, I imagine) wonders aloud about the couple below in 5A, suggesting it's time to invite us for dinner. After all, she says, they *are* our neighbors. Neighbors that could become friends.

⌒∞⌒

When I first phoned my older brother in California to confirm that, yes, the family rumors were true, that Donald and I were indeed selling our house in North Carolina to move to a furnished sublet in Midtown Manhattan, Tom was quiet for a moment. I could sense what was coming. Like almost everyone else—our friends, neighbors, family members—he was going to tell us we were making a mistake. A big mistake. To move to the city at our ages? Without jobs lined up?

I had my stock answer ready: "It's an adventure. We've

saved enough to last two years. If we don't find work by then, we'll move back."

I heard Tom's sigh, the intake of breath before he spoke. "It won't be like Seinfeld, you know."

"Seinfeld?" I tried to sound surprised, as if I had no idea what he was suggesting. What he meant, of course, was that our new life would not be a sitcom. Friends and neighbors wouldn't be dropping in, flopping down on the sofa, warming the cold rooms with their witticisms and eccentric charm. "Time will tell," I answered briskly.

"I just don't want you to be disappointed. Hey, it's your big brother talking here."

"I know," I said. "But I've got to get back to my packing."

After I hung up the phone, I finished taping up the few boxes we would be taking with us. To Apartment 5A. Yes, Tom, 5A. The same apartment number as Jerry Seinfeld's. So there.

⁂

I've always hated signing guest books—at art openings, weddings, B&Bs—especially those that require a comment. Even worse are the books that people plant on their entry hall tables or in the guest room, beside the bed they so generously provide for you. You can't simply sign your name; that would signal ingratitude. You're expected to say something nice. The pressure is on.

So, given my distaste for such traditions, why did I keep a guest book all those years in North Carolina and then pack it up to take to New York? As guest books go, it's a beautiful one, filled with line drawings of mansions and cottages alongside quotations from Shakespeare, Byron, Charlotte

Brontë, and other writers. We chose the Jane Austen page for our first New York guests to sign, with its quotation from *Persuasion*: ". . . they all went in-doors with their new friends, and found rooms so small as none but those who invite from the heart could think capable of accommodating so many."

Yes, I decided as I placed the book on the landlords' coffee table, my mind glittering with domestic scenarios. Yes, I will invite from the heart. Blessings on all who enter here. May these rooms overflow with new friends.

The rooms have indeed overflowed. All five of my siblings have visited, along with two nieces, two nephews, Donald's son and his girlfriend, our sprawling, out-of-state family filling the foldout sofa, the futon, and the guest book: "We came, we ate, we drank, we blistered!" But no new friends. A few New York acquaintances have come for dinner, promising in their guest book comments that we'll get together again soon, that this is the start of a beautiful friendship, that "We can hang out like Lucy & Ethel & Ricky & Fred—Babaloo!"

Months later, it still hasn't happened. Where are my Kramers and Georges and Elaines and Jerrys? Friends who will drop by unannounced, walk with Donald and me in the park, invite us from the heart into their small rooms?

⌘

The aria our 5B neighbor sang that first day sounded familiar. From *Don Giovanni*, I believe, though my opera knowledge is so rusty that I can't be sure. Throughout the summer, he's rehearsed other arias I can't name, in German and Italian. Then one afternoon in early September, he segues into

Handel ("Behold, I tell you a mystery") and with the first few measures I'm on home turf again, my memory opening wide enough to mute the piano plunking out notes and to imagine the orchestral bridge between recitative and aria until, here it comes, and I close my eyes as his voice breaks through—"The trumpet shall sound, and the dead shall be raised incorruptible."

That does it—I have to thank him. Yes, of course, and then invite him for dinner! I wait until he finishes the session and the piano cover closes. Hurry before you lose your nerve, I think, but Jesus I look terrible, I'm in my writing clothes, the stretched-out sweats, and what kind of first impression would that make? So I rush into jeans, choose a green sweater I hope will accent my eyes, swipe some lip gloss across my chapped lips, and hurry out into the hall, just as he is locking his door.

"Excuse me," I say.

He jerks—I've startled him—and turns from the door. He's wearing a flat cap with a small bill, the kind of cap Donald wears. His eyes are dark and kind. I introduce myself. He smiles and nods politely. "Pleased to meet you." His speaking voice is deep and sonorous, as I'd imagined it would be.

"I just have to tell you how much I love your singing."

His eyes narrow, his brow furrows. "You can hear me? I tried to choose a time when no one is home." His voice tightens with each word.

"You don't understand," I say. "I love hearing it. It makes my day."

"I'm so sorry. How awful. To bother a neighbor. That's the worst thing. I'll try to keep it down."

"Please don't," I say. "It's the highlight of my day." My

first face-to-face encounter with a neighbor, and I'm blow-ing it royally.

His lips lift into something approximating a smile. He's probably thinking, Poor woman, if this is the highlight of her day. "Okay," he says. "Okay, then." He walks briskly to-ward the elevator and punches the button. "I'm late for re-hearsal. Nice to meet you."

⁓

Thus continues my education in New York apartment dwelling: never let your neighbors know that you can hear them through the walls. Apparently this qualifies as invasion of privacy.

But what about cookies? Chocolate chip, who could re-sist? I decide on the traditional Toll House, doubling the recipe for good luck—I could feed the whole fifth floor! Af-ter arranging several cookies on a plate, I step out into the warm, cookie-scented hallway. The singer isn't home yet, so I knock on 5D, the apartment that sometimes smells like baking bread. I knock, wait. Hear footsteps approaching, stopping. Surely they can see me through the peephole. I knock again, wait. Hear footsteps retreating.

Move on to 5F, the curry-turmeric neighbor. There's a television in the background, some kind of shoot-'em-up. Knock, knock. Footsteps approaching, stopping. A lock clicking, another lock, another. The door opens a few inch-es, the security chain still latched. "What is it?" a gruff voice growls. "What's the problem?"

"No problem. Just cookies." My voice is a squeak. "From your neighbor in 5A."

"Thanks but no thanks." Door closes.

The cookies are cooling by the minute. I think of the painter in 4A, but I don't want to disturb him if he's working. And the couple in 6A? I haven't heard their toilet flushing for days now; they must be traveling. If only it were meter-reading day, I know the Con Ed guy would take a handful. I stand in the hallway a long time, looking down at the cookies on the white plate, one of the plates the landlords left for us. Jesus, I don't even have my own plates. They're in North Carolina, too. Along with my family, our friends, our house—no, not *our* house, it belongs to someone else now. Our cat too. How could we have given up our cat?

The cookies are cooling, my tears are coming hard. This is it. This is my life. And I am so lonely.

◦◦◦

The morning after the cookie incident, I phone two writer acquaintances, native New Yorkers, to explain what happened.

"Oh no," says the first one. "Never do that. A Manhattan apartment is a sacred space. A sanctuary."

"You don't just drop by," says the second. "Always phone ahead. Make arrangements."

"Like a play date?" I ask. "But that seems silly. I mean, everyone's so close."

"Exactly," she says. "And that door is all that keeps you from the chaos outside."

It will be years from this moment before I understand that veteran New Yorkers have a different relationship with doors, and with "the chaos outside," than newcomers do. Having built a personal history in the city, they are so firmly ensconced in their neighborhoods and apartment buildings, their lives so rich in social connections, that they need to keep the chaos out. Because it is always trying to get in.

But at this moment, as I thank my informants and hang up the phone, all I can think is, Chaos? What are you talking about? No chaos is knocking at our door.

Unless you count the Con Ed guy, who arrives the first week of each month to read our meter. His song ("Gas Man! Gas Man!") begins as he steps out of the elevator and continues into the hall. On his first visit, I waited for a knock at our door, but now as soon as I hear "Gas Man!" I hurry to greet him, motioning him inside before he can even knock. He's a tall, fleshy black man who wears his weight well; my grandmother would have called him "portly." His short-trimmed hair is salt-and-pepper, like his beard, but it's his broad smile that defines him, and his eyes, crinkling at the edges.

"Are you always this cheerful?" I asked the first morning, after I'd led him into the kitchen where the meter is housed.

"Mostly, yes," he said. "I go to bed that way and wake up that way, and if I ever start feeling otherwise, the noise I make in the hallway clears it all out."

"It's not noise," I said. "It's music."

He nodded appreciatively. "Well, I asked the doctor and he said, 'That's just fine, just keep making that noise.'"

Since that day, I try to keep something sweet in one of the tins our landlords left—brownies, fig bars, cookies. Sometimes he takes two or three; oatmeal is his favorite. I'd ask him to sign the guest book, but I don't want to risk written evidence in case Con Ed has rules against employee-customer relationships. Though I hope I'm more than a customer to him by now. Last month, when he noticed the scoreboard on our fridge ("Mice vs. Humans") and saw by the tally that the mice were winning the latest round, he nodded sympathetically.

"I plan to get a cat," I said, explaining my recent trips to the animal shelter and several pet stores. "But the one I really want is back in North Carolina." His eyebrows lifted in interest, all the invitation I needed, and before I could stop myself I'd told him the whole story—selling the house, giving away our cat, leaving our friends and family. I offered him a brownie, and as he headed out the door, he suggested stuffing steel wool in the baseboard cracks. So far, his advice appears sound. Humans have taken the lead.

∽∾

Last month, a soprano moved in with the baritone. The day she arrived, their door was propped open while they carried in boxes from the lobby, and when I heard them enter the elevator I stepped out into the hallway to investigate. One box was marked "clothes" and another "shoes." A third, open box was filled with vinyl LPs. I'd known that 5B was a small studio, but I had no idea just *how* small until I peeked in the door. A baby grand piano nearly filled the long, narrow space. The only interior door, which had to be the door to the bathroom, was closed, clearing my visual field so that I could see all the way to the window, the only window, under which a narrow bed was placed. She must be small, I figured, smaller even than the baritone; otherwise, the shared bed would be a very tight fit.

The soprano practices in the morning, so my days are going well—there's nothing like joy to distract you from writing. The timbre of her voice is warm and bright, surprisingly velvety on the legato. She sounds younger than the baritone, probably in her late twenties, about the age of my eldest niece. Sometimes I hear her moving around in the apartment after the baritone has left. One morning I heard crying—soft, muffled sobs—coming from behind the wall. Maybe she's new to the city. Maybe she's missing her sisters, her nieces, her friends. Maybe she likes cookies.

‹∞›

It's been unusually quiet below us lately, and cigarette smoke no longer filters up through the plaster. The painter in 4A must have moved out. So much for the gallery opening. As for the couple in 6A, things don't look hopeful in that department either. Though I still haven't glimpsed the male counterpart (if there is one) I believe I've correctly identified the mystery woman. Because of a moderate case of claustrophobia, I rarely use the elevator, but earlier this morning my rolling cart was too filled with groceries for me to handle the stairs. A woman in the lobby held the elevator door for me. A short, buxom, coffee-with-cream-complexioned woman about my age, she's a stylish dresser, if I can judge from the luxurious red cape.

Once we were in the elevator, she punched the button for floor six. I punched button five, turning to give her a smile. "We're 5A," I said, hoping she'd reply in kind. "You're welcome to stop by for a drink anytime."

She nodded but did not speak.

"5A," I repeated. "Easy to remember. Seinfeld's apartment, you know."

The elevator stopped at the fifth floor and the door opened. "Well then, this is me, my floor," I said, maneuvering my loaded cart out into the hallway. That's when I noticed her cane. Of course, I thought. A cane. That accounts for the rhythmic tap-tapping I hear throughout the day. But I would never mention that; I've learned my lesson.

Now inside the apartment, I unload the cart of groceries, listening for the soprano to begin warming up. I've bought a dozen yellow roses from the greengrocer on the corner, as I do every week. Yellow always lifts my spirits. But it's the grocer himself that keeps me going back. I'm a regular now. When I enter, he nods and moves out from behind the counter to select the freshest bouquet. Sometimes he ties it with a ribbon.

From next door, the piano sounds its first tentative notes and the soprano's voice sifts through the wall. I arrange the roses in a tall crystal vase and place it on the table opposite the mirror, doubling the profusion of yellow blooms. The woman in the mirror looks back at me. Her eyes are bright, she seems almost happy—when did that happen, when had the tears stopped? I can't see past this moment, and in this moment, I don't want to know what the future holds.

As it turns out, the couple in 5B will never sign our guest book. They will never enter our apartment and we will never enter theirs. In the elevator one day, I will introduce myself to the soprano, but I won't mention the singing because I don't want it to stop. Her voice will fill my mornings for many months and the baritone's voice will fill my afternoons.

Months will grow into years, past the trauma and grief of the 9/11 attacks, through three seasons of *Messiah* and two spring concerts. Then one morning years into our separate, shared future, I will return from a walk in the park and see two boxes outside the door of 5B—"clothes" and "shoes"—and later that morning, as I wait for the soprano's music to begin, I will hear the crying. But this time it is not muffled and it does not stop. This well is deep, fathomless, the sobs rising to an anguished howl like the howl of an animal caught in a trap.

What comes next will stay with me for years to come, arriving in memory with the sting of present-tense clarity:

Wait, the howl is stopping. I hear footsteps moving quietly across their floor—is she barefoot? The click of a lock, the front door opening, and the thump of something heavy landing in the hallway between our doors: her box of LPs? The door closes again and the crying begins anew, but softer now, and softer still, diminishing to a whimper.

I go to the kitchen and reach for the cookie tin. I've been saving the extras for the Con Ed guy to share with his grandkids, but I know he'll understand. I arrange five or six on the landlord's white plate, walk into the hallway, and knock. Behind the wall, footsteps are moving toward me. A lock is clicking, the door opening. The young woman stands in the doorway, wearing a wrinkled blue kimono sashed loosely at the waist. Her dark hair is mussed. Her feet are bare. She looks down at the packing boxes and the box of LPs as if seeing them for the first time. I nod, shrug. My eyes are stinging, tears starting—not for me, I realize in surprise, but for her. Her eyes, heavily lashed and smeared with mascara, look directly into mine. I hold out the plate and she reaches to take it.

Book Marks

I AM WORRIED ABOUT the woman. I am afraid she might hurt herself, perhaps has already hurt herself—there's no way to know which of the return dates stamped on the book of poems is hers. The book, Denise Levertov's *Evening Train*, belongs to the New York Public Library. I checked it out yesterday and can keep it for three weeks. Studying the clues readers leave in books is one of my obsessions—tracking the evidence and guessing the lives beneath. Even as my reasonable mind is having its say (How can you assume, the marks could have been made by anyone, for any reason, over any period of time…) my other self is leaving on its own journey.

There's no way to know for certain that the phantom library patron is a woman, but all signs point in that direction. On one page is a red smear that looks like lipstick, and between two other pages, lying like a bookmark, is a long, graying hair. The underlinings, which may or may not have been made by the woman, are in pencil—pale, tentative marks I study carefully, reverently, the way an archaeologist traces a fossil's delicate imprint. The rest is dream, conjecture, the making of *my* story. I've always been a hungry reader, what one of my friends calls a "selfish reader." "Is there any other kind?" I asked my friend. "Don't we all read to answer our own needs, to point us toward some light?"

Ever since we moved to the city, I've been homesick for my books, the hundreds of volumes stored in my brother's basement in North Carolina. I miss having them near me, running my hands over their spines, recalling when and where I acquired each one, and out of what need. Sometimes when I'm working at my desk, I forget for a minute where I am, turning in my chair to reach for Neruda, say, or Kumin or Heaney or Akhmatova, only to be jolted back into the present moment, into our Midtown sublet furnished with everything the owners assumed we would need. Except books.

Thus my frequent visits to the New York Public Library. The Beaux Arts main branch on Fifth Avenue is the most beautiful, but since it's not a lending library, I spend most of my time at our neighborhood branch, where the reference librarian is a local treasure. When I'm working at home, I phone her whenever I'm marooned in the middle of a paragraph that requires knowledge outside my field; that would be almost everything. Sometimes I make up excuses to call, just to hear a human voice. Especially the voice of someone who, like me, gets excited over a word like *matryoshka*.

"It's the name for those Russian nesting dolls," I explained one morning, "like you see in the craft booths outside the Metropolitan. I've seen several different spellings, but I need the right one."

"Hold on," she said. "Wait a minute. I see a Slav walking toward me right now. I'll ask him." Only in New York, right? So the librarian did exactly that, she asked the Slav, which is why I was able to correctly type *matryoshka* a few paragraphs back.

Moments like these are only one of many reasons why I love librarians. Carolyn, my mother's closest friend and a childhood mentor, was a librarian. She not only loved books, she believed in them, the way Great Aunt Bessie believed in them but even more so. Carolyn believed that books could change our lives, could save us from ourselves.

Some of the underlinings in *Evening Train* have been partially erased (eraser crumbles have gathered in the center seams) as if the woman reconsidered her first responses or tried to cover her tracks. The markings do not strike me as those of a defiant woman but rather the markings of one who has not only taken her blows but feels she deserves them. She has underlined "serviceable heart" in one poem; in another, "Greyhaired, I have not grown wiser." If she exists, I would like to sit down with this woman. We seem to have a lot in common. We chose the same book, we both wear red lipstick, and though I am not as honest as the woman (the gray in my hair is hidden beneath an auburn rinse) I am probably her age or thereabouts.

And judging from what she has left on the pages of Levertov's poems, it appears that our hearts have worn down in the same places. This is the part that worries me. Though my serviceable heart mended years ago, hers seems to be in the very act of breaking. A present-tense pain pulses through each marked-up poem, and the more pages I turn, the clearer it becomes what she is considering. I want to reach through the pages and lead her out through another door.

⚬∞⚬

Over the course of many years, Carolyn gave me books she felt I needed for navigating difficult passages in my life. She shared my passion for hand-me-downs and never apologized for giving me used books. "Words don't go bad like cheese," she'd say. "Read everything you can get your hands on. Live inside the books!" On the subject of my newfound love, she was even more adamant. "You're too young to give it all up for a man. Especially that man." Like Carolyn, Great Aunt Bessie was outspoken on the matter of my forthcoming wedding to Peter. Both women had married older, stable, kind men who allowed them the space their inquiring minds demanded. "I'm afraid you're going to lose yourself," Aunt Bessie told me.

Studying the markings in *Evening Train*, I surmise that the gray-haired woman is an honest reader, unashamed to admit her ignorance. She has drawn boxes around difficult words—*epiphanies, antiphonal, tessellations, serrations*—and placed large question marks above each box. Maybe she's merely an eager learner, the kind who sets small tasks for herself: she will go directly to the dictionary and find these words. Or maybe someone—her lover, her husband, whoever broke her serviceable heart—also criticized her vocabulary. It was too small or too large. She asked too many questions.

In the poem about the breaking heart, the woman has underlined "in surface fissures" and "a web / of hairline fractures." She probably didn't even notice the fissures at first. Maybe, she guessed, this webbing is the necessary landscape of every marriage, each act of love. But reading on, I sense that more has been broken than a metaphorical heart. She has circled the entire poem "The Batterers," about a man who, after beating a woman, dresses her wounds and, in the act, begins to love her again: "Why had he never / seen, before, what she was? / What if she stops breathing?"

I tell myself I wouldn't have stayed in that kind of situation. As it is, I'll never know what I would have done.

Peter never hit me, though one night, desperate for attention, to be *seen*, I dared him to. (How do we live with the knowledge of our past selves?) Maybe the gray-haired woman, like the poem's narrator, and like me, is unable to call forth the face of the one she finally left, who had first left her. Why else mark these lines: "the shape / of his head, or / color of his eyes appear / at moments, but I can't / assemble feature with feature"?

When I am in pain I devour books, stripping the words of conceptual and metaphorical context and digging straight for the meat. The gray-haired woman seems to be doing the same, taking each word personally, *too* personally, as if Levertov had written them expressly for her, to guide her toward some terrible action. Certainly this wasn't Levertov's intention, yet the more I study the markings, the more I fear what the woman is considering. In the poem "Dream Instruction" she has underlined, twice, "gradual stillness" but appears to have missed entirely the "blessing" in the lines that follow.

The marks in "Contraband" are even more alarming. I want to take the woman by the hand and remind her of the poem's symbolic level, a level that's nearly impossible to see when you are in pain. "Contraband," I would tell her, is a symbol for the tree of knowledge, the tree of reason, and the fruit is the words we stuff into our mouths, and yes, that fruit might indeed be "toxic in large quantities; fumes / swirled in our heads and around us," but those lines are not a prescription for suicide. There are other ways to live with knowledge.

The narrator of *Evening Train* seems to have found a way: she sets off on a journey. Though I suspect that the luggage and racks of the book's title poem are metaphorical, I can't help but feel the heft of the bags, the steel slickness of the racks. And as I study the phantom woman's markings, it seems clear that, like my journey nearly three decades ago, her journey required a real ticket on a real train or plane, and that by the time she had arrived at the poem called "Arrived," she had already sat alone in a room with "Chairs, / sofa, table, a cup" and begun the inventory of her life—a life, she may soon decide, that is no longer worth the trouble.

∞

Two years before Donald and I moved to New York, when Carolyn's cancer had metastasized and she could count the remaining months on her fingers, she wrote to me from her home in Virginia asking me to come as soon as possible to help sort through her books. "All I ask is that you don't cry. Come early, stay late. And leave with your arms full."

We spent two afternoons going through the books. Too weak to stand, Carolyn sat on a little stool, pointing and nodding, directing me shelf by shelf. Each row called forth a memory. Book by book, her life's story unfolded, and, as she spoke, her story folded seamlessly into mine. She was glad that our lives had touched, glad I had survived the darkest years and found a husband this time who was good to me. Then she handed me a large envelope, explaining that one of her jobs as librarian had been to inspect the returned books before re-shelving them. "You'd be surprised at what people use as bookmarks," she said.

When I got home, I emptied the envelope onto the floor, amazed at what spilled out. Bits and pieces of strangers' lives, hundreds of markers of personal histories. Love letters, folded place mats, envelopes, sympathy cards, valentines, handwritten recipes, train tickets, report cards, newspaper clippings, certificates of achievement, bills, receipts, religious tracts, swimming pool passes, scratch-and-sniff perfume ads, cancelled tickets for the bullfight, bar coasters, rice paper, happy money. Studying the bookmarks, I slid into each stranger's life, wondering which book he had checked out from the library and whether he had finished it.

I smooth the center seam of *Evening Train* and run my hands over the marked-up lines. Poems can be dangerous places in which to venture alone, and I'm not sure the woman is ready for "After *Mindwalk*." She has underlined "panic's black cloth falling / over our faces, over our breath." Please don't, I want to say. Don't do it. Look, see the footnote? *Mindwalk* was a film by Bernt Capra; it's not a real place. It's about Pascal and the Void. It doesn't have to be about you.

But it is, of course. That's why she is not only reading the book but also writing one of her own, with each scratch of the pencil. The printed words are Levertov's, but the other poem is the woman's—written in the margins, in the small boxes that cage the words she cannot pronounce, in the crumbled erasures, in the question marks floating above the lines. Wait up, I want to say—a crazy thought, but I can't help myself. Wait up, I want to tell you something.

Hello Stranger

ON THE PARK BENCH opposite mine, two women tilt their heads in conversation. Their ages are hard to guess, especially that of the small woman dressed like a Catholic school child: pleated skirt, Mary Jane flats, a black bow anchoring a pageboy too thick and shiny not to be a wig. Her legs are so short that her feet don't touch the ground, and the Mary Janes swing back and forth. The other woman is large, her body an awkward assembly of unmatched parts, something a committee might put together.

"So, how much do you pay?" asks the small woman. Her voice is high and chirpy.

The large woman mumbles something I can't make out.

"So," Small Woman continues, "is that gas and electric? Well, then, that's good, good." She adjusts her hair bow and smooths the pleats on her skirt. There is a long pause. "How do they clean cows anyway? I mean, is milk safe? How can they keep it clean? Humans are the same way; it can't be good for the babies."

Large Woman nods.

"They can't fix the TV," chirps Small Woman.

"How many do you have?" Large Woman's voice is deep, with the throaty rasp of a longtime smoker.

"A big one, medium-sized one, a little one. It's the little one."

"It's the tubes. It's always the tubes."

"I tell you, it can't be fixed. They said so."

"There's nothing wrong with that TV," says Large Woman. "Pull out the old tubes. It'll be good as new."

There is another long pause. Finally, Small Woman speaks. "I'm lonely. Where are all my friends?"

Large Woman turns to look at Small Woman, but Small Woman does not return her gaze. "What about the dancer?" she offers.

"Who?" chirps Small Woman.

"The dancer. The dancer, the dancer!"

"Oh, her." Another long pause. "I'm lonely."

A look of pain crosses Large Woman's face—briefly, then it's gone—and I'm thinking Small Woman should look at Large Woman, pat her hand, something. After all, Small Woman isn't alone, she's got Large Woman, doesn't *she* count? She's there right beside her. She should count.

Or is she too close to count, too common a sight for Small Woman to appreciate? Common makes no splash; only rare stops us. The air around my park bench is alive with bird chatter, squawk, rasp that I might name *song* if I did not hear it every single morning. And yesterday, hundreds of perfect ginkgo leaves were scattered at my feet. Had there been only one, I would have stooped to pick it up. I might have taken it home and framed it. The ginkgo tree is Chinese in origin, but Chinese tourists never photograph the ginkgos. They photograph New York squirrels; New Yorkers don't.

Maybe living in a great city is like being in a long friendship. Why look at the woman beside you on the bench.

She'll be there tomorrow. Why visit Ellis Island, the Statue of Liberty, the World Trade Center. Why grab this moment when there will always be another moment like it, and another. What is that old saying about there being only two stories? Someone goes on a journey or a stranger comes to town. Maybe it takes a stranger to wake you up—to your city, your loved ones, your life.

Hello, Stranger.

"And We Shall Be Changed":
September 7–11, 2001

Friday, September 7

WE'RE AT THE BREAKFAST table, the new cat Leila curled on the chair between us. Donald has almost finished his bagel, but I'm still groggy—the second cup of coffee hasn't yet kicked in—and I'm staring at the living room window, admiring, in a bleary sort of way, the white gauze curtain we recently draped across the top. I look around the room, studying the few possessions we brought with us from North Carolina: the theater posters, my grandmother's afghan, the painting of a long-necked woman standing beside a peacock. I fantasize about planting something in the clay pots our landlords left behind, still filled with soil, on the tiny Juliet balcony.

The white curtain softens the view of high-rise offices and gives the illusion of privacy, although I know the office workers across the street can see us because we can see them. White is impractical, of course, what with the exhaust fumes from the Sixth Avenue buses and the steam from the ancient radiator, but the sheer curtain allows for at least a touch of light. Light is what I've missed most since we moved to the city. Although sun shines on much of New York—Central Park is sun-flooded, as is much of the Village, and the light scattering across the Hudson can hurt your eyes—here in Midtown, in the canyon of skyscrapers, sun peeks through our apartment shyly, for an hour a day at most.

When the first signs of light appear, I get up from my writing desk and move to the green rug, where Leila is already stretched out. I lie beside her on my back, kick off my shoes, let the brightness pour over my face, my feet. Some days I think of my family and friends in North Carolina, the house we sold so that we could afford a furnished sublet here, the hundred-year-old oaks that shaded our yard, the lost garden and its changing light.

But most days I just say thank you to no one in particular, for this city, for the miracle of millions of toilets flushing all at once, for cheap, abundant flowers and unidentifiable produce on street corners, for the rich broth of languages I hear on my walks, for the public library where the checkout clerk stands on a stool, a woman with thalidomide sprouts for arms and a scar down the side of her face, who stamps whatever book I bring to her without asking any questions. New York is a great place to be noticed or not to be noticed, to find yourself or lose yourself, depending on what you need. Once, walking in Central Park, I saw what looked like several small paddleboats floating in the South Pond. They turned out to be part of an installation titled *A–Z Deserted Islands*. The artist had anchored them so that they maintained a comfortable distance from each other without ever touching. The boats seemed to me then and seem to me now to be the perfect metaphor for New York City. Isolation is what makes living here possible. An island can be a refuge, like those islands in the middle of an intersection that keep you safe until the traffic clears.

I look across the table at Donald. He's brushing crumbs

from his robe; he brings grace to the most ordinary gesture. It's one of many things I admire about him—his easy elegance, the serene way he adapts to any situation. He stands to clear the table when suddenly, what was that? A noisy scatter, a crash, a hectic scramble too sudden to trace, and, in a flurry of fur and claws, Leila leaps from the chair and heads for the fireplace, where something dark is skittering across the metal grate, across the floor toward the bedroom. Then a squeal, a screech, and Leila skids around the corner. A mouse, I think for an instant—we've had mice before—but no, this was too large, with a sweeping tail. Now it darts from the bedroom toward the front window, leaping onto the white curtain, the theater posters, the peacock painting, then down again, across the floor and into the kitchen.

Donald runs interference while I corral Leila into the bedroom and shut the door, then rush to call the super, a handsome, dark-eyed immigrant from Montenegro whose young wife and five children live in the basement of the building. "A squirrel dropped into the apartment!" I shriek. "What should we do?"

He answers calmly, as if he's been saving the answer for years: "Open a window."

Which I promptly do, and within minutes the squirrel has leapt up to the sill and out to the balcony. I close the window and turn to Donald. "A squirrel," he says, shaking his head in disbelief. "Down the chimney."

"A wounded squirrel," I say, pointing to several drops of blood on the sill.

"On the wall too."

I glance at the wall above the sofa where the theater posters have been knocked askew: smears of squirrel blood. And dark red spatters on the peacock woman painting and on the gauze curtain. Donald heads for the kitchen. When he returns, sponge in hand, he quietly reports that there's blood there, too, on the floor, the cabinets. We try out scenarios: was the squirrel injured in the fall, or did he scuffle with Leila? How did he get down the chimney in the first place? There are five floors above us, five other fireplaces into which he might have dropped. Five below us too. Why ours? And what was he doing on the roof of a Midtown building, anyway? The park is several blocks away, across two busy intersections.

After cleaning up the blood spatters, Donald showers and dresses. We check the balcony, where the squirrel has burrowed into one of the clay pots. "He needs to rest," Donald says, reaching for his satchel. I confirm our plans to meet after work at the International Center of Photography. These are the last few days of Sebastião Salgado's exhibit *Migrations*, and I don't want to miss it. After Donald leaves, I release Leila from the bedroom—no sign of blood on her whiskers, her paws—and after a few minutes, she settles into one of her favorite spaces, the edge of my desk, atop a manuscript. I put on my writing uniform—old shorts, T-shirt, slippers. Years ago, I learned that if I dress in my worst clothes and don't comb my hair, I won't be tempted to go out for a paper or a bagel but will get straight to work and stay at the desk longer.

The traffic on the avenue is roaring, but the air in the apartment is stale and close, so I crack the window a few inches, switch my white noise machine to the forest setting, and sharpen a pencil. Suddenly Leila hisses, lifts her head. I glance to my left. The squirrel is squirming through the open window, his dark glassy eyes darting side to side. I run to the window, shoo him back out and slam the window, hard.

That's when it comes to me: the squirrel has nowhere else to go. He's trapped on the balcony, five stories above the street. Inches from me, he's trembling, raised up on his back legs, his wounded paw held tightly against his pale gray chest. Leila hisses, moves toward the window. The squirrel crawls back into the clay pot. I pick up the phone and call the super, who says he has no idea where the squirrel came from. "Don't touch it," he says, as if I would touch a squirrel. I've heard the stories—I know they can be vicious when attacked, not to mention rabid. They're fiercely territorial. The super advises me to call "the city." I know what that means, so I decide to wait and talk it over with Donald tonight. The squirrel might be dead by then anyway. He already looks dead, curled in the pot in fetal position, or what I imagine a squirrel's fetal position to be. With his head and feet tucked out of sight and his tail encircling his body, he resembles a Daniel Boone cap. He's breathing, but barely.

∽∞∽

The sky is still light as we step out of the exhibit and onto the street. I feel dazed, stunned by Salgado's images: worn faces, bent backs, crowded boats and wagons, packed train cars stalled on tracks, veiled women, starving children peeking out from beneath filthy blankets, one-legged men struggling down rubble-strewn streets. Traveling for seven years in forty-seven countries, Salgado documented the global cycle of displacement and migration. His artist's statement articulates his goal: "I hope that the person who comes into my show and the person who comes out are not quite the same." Walking up Sixth Avenue, Donald silent beside me, the Dow Jones end-of-week losses scrolling in neon two stories above our heads, I wonder aloud how our city has escaped the sort of devastation so many others have recently suffered. Donald shrugs: "Just lucky, I guess." But nothing stays the same forever, he reminds me.

That was Salgado's message too. Cities like New York and London and Paris, Salgado said in a recent interview, are now "the towns of the past." The "towns of the future" are Manila, Bombay, São Paulo, cities that used to have four or five million people but now have fifteen million or more. Migrants follow the food source, literally and figuratively. They're running not only from something but also toward something—call it opportunity, progress, a new start. That's why Donald's grandparents settled in New York after emigrating from Russia by way of Switzerland, then Canada, then Chicago. It's why my friend's ancestors came from Poland, and why my paternal grandfather, as a child, walked with his mother and younger brother into central Illinois, carrying their possessions on their backs. Salgado was born on a farm in Brazil, moved to a small city when he was five, to a larger city when he was fifteen, then to the metropolis of São Paulo, and then, for political reasons, to France. "Today," he says, "I am still a foreign person living in a foreign country."

When we return home, Donald goes directly to the window to check on the squirrel, who's still curled up in the pot. He appears to be breathing, though it may just be the breeze ruffling the fur on his tail. Leila, no longer stationed by the window in alert mode, has returned to her accustomed spot on the sofa. Donald pours us each a Scotch and fills a small bowl with peanuts, his nightly treat. Before we go to bed, we agree that if the squirrel is still alive tomorrow, we'll figure out a plan.

Saturday, September 8

In the morning, the pot is empty. We peer into the other clay pots and visually search the balcony. No sign of the squirrel. Donald opens the window a little, just far enough to position a hand mirror aimed at our neighbors' window. "He's there," he says. Our neighbors in 5B have a small studio apartment that doesn't have a Juliet balcony, only a ledge two or three inches wide. An amazing feat, I think, especially considering the wounded paw—leaping the five or six feet between our windows, several stories above a busy street, and landing on a narrow ledge. I feel relieved. If he can get to their ledge, maybe he can get to another one, and another. Maybe he can escape. But to where? The street below, furious with buses, taxis, and foot traffic, half a mile from the nearest tree?

Well, now it's our neighbors' problem. I feel a twinge of guilt mixed with jealousy. They'll probably find a way to rescue him. They seem like the kind of people who will do the right thing. They're opera singers, and we've never heard anything but beautiful sounds come through the wall we share. Even her sneezes are lovely, inspired, and their practice sessions are welcome interruptions to my writing day. Soon it will be time for him to start rehearsing the baritone solo for *Messiah*, which he performs every holiday season. It's one of my favorite arias, and I always stop what I'm working on to listen: "And the dead shall be raised incorruptible . . . In a moment, in the twinkling of an eye . . . And we shall be changed." Anyone who can sing like that can certainly rescue a squirrel.

Then I remember that we haven't heard any sounds from

the apartment for days. They must be traveling again, and who knows for how long this time? Days, weeks? The squirrel could starve by then, or dehydrate. It's bad enough if he dies from a wound, but I have no control over that. Starvation would definitely be on my conscience. I tell Donald that we need to do something, lure him back to our balcony.

"Put some water out," he says.

"I was thinking maybe peanuts."

"My peanuts? My cocktail peanuts?"

"We can get more peanuts," I say.

"If you feed something, it will stay."

"I know." I lean over and kiss him on top of his head. "You're still here, right?"

That weakens him. "Okay, but don't use a good bowl." All the dishes in the apartment belong to our landlords, and in the past few weeks I've broken two. I find some plastic soup containers from the Chinese take-out, fill one with water and the other with peanuts, and slip them through the open window, beside the large clay pot.

"Squirrels aren't pets. Just remember that," he says.

I could mention the albino squirrel my great-grandfather kept in his farmhouse for months, but I don't want to push my luck. "Just for the time being," I say. "Until we can think of something."

I close the window, change into my walking shoes, and head out for the park. I walk there at least four times a week, usually in early afternoon—past the baseball fields, the playground, the benches where the homeless gather beneath a canopy of hardwood trees lush with bird song and squirrel chatter. Central Park squirrels are descendants of wild squirrels that lived in this area's forests before the city was founded. They're amazingly adaptable, surviving in an environment not only alien but sometimes hostile. A hundred years ago, when the park squirrel population reached one thousand, park officials hired marksmen to shoot about three hundred of them—at close range, so the story goes. But the squirrels came back stronger than ever, thousands upon thousands of them, and they keep thriving. They follow the food source—not just the acorns and seeds scrounged from trees and bushes but also scraps dropped by human hands. Maybe that's how my squirrel (when did I start calling him mine?) came to us. Maybe he followed a trail of nuts or seeds from the edge of the park, across Fifty-Ninth Street, Fifty-Eighth, Fifty-Seventh, Fifty-Sixth, darting between buses, taxis, and then, when he saw that the food trail had ended, he went the direction squirrels usually go: up. Perhaps up the scaffolding that for two years surrounded the apartment building adjacent to ours.

Walking back, I turn the corner onto our street and look up to see if he's returned to our balcony. But no, he's clinging to the neighbor's window ledge, his tail quivering, his head tilted down toward the sidewalk as if considering his fate. Is a squirrel capable of weighing options? He seems to be, glancing now to the street below, now over to our balcony. Can he smell the soil in the clay pot? Maybe his nose remembers the dirt where he burrowed last night. The wind is picking up. If he knows what's good for him, he'll come back to our side.

But what if he decides there's no way out but down? "Look," I say in desperation, grabbing the arm of the gray-haired man who's sweeping the sidewalk outside our building. Startled, he turns to me. I don't know the man's name, but he resembles our super—perhaps an uncle—and I've seen him inside the building, emptying garbage cans, wrapping the cardboard recyclables with twine. I point to the ledge: "There's a squirrel up there." The man smiles nervously, the kind of smile you give to feral-looking people on the subway, to humor them long enough to make your escape.

I point again, more vehemently this time, but the man just shrugs. "No English," he says. Maybe he's only recently arrived in the city, like the super's younger brother, who helped out last year. I haven't seen an older woman, so maybe he came here alone and now lives with the super's family. I've never been in their apartment, but I've seen all the shoes stacked neatly on shoe racks outside the door: men's work boots, children's sneakers, women's and girls' clogs in the latest fashion.

The man shrugs apologetically and goes back to his sweeping. Of course he goes back to his sweeping. What else can he do? English or no English, he's as helpless as I am. From this vantage point, there's nothing else to be done—short of fashioning a squirrel rescue net, an option I actually consider for an instant in a flash of cartoon logic that quickly burns itself out, replaced by an equally ridiculous yet very real instinct of, what? Tenderness? A feeling of maternal responsibility for this little rat-like creature? He looks so small and vulnerable, so visibly terrified, against the backdrop of the city buildings.

I hurry up the stairs—because of my claustrophobia I avoid elevators whenever I can—and look up the phone number for the animal control department. After all, I *am* a taxpayer, and for all they know, the squirrel could be a pet that escaped while I was cleaning windows. I'm sure they've heard stranger stories. They've got the equipment, the know-how. Surely they'll have a plan. I dial the number. A recorded voice tells me to push "one" for English, then another voice tells me that all lines are busy and I should just be patient. Soft music starts up, a third recorded voice tells me it won't be long now, and then a real live voice comes on. The man sounds very young, with a smooth foreign accent. I start in on the story I've rehearsed—about my pet squirrel who's trapped on the balcony—but the man is responding so sympathetically, with just the right amount of "yesses," "hmmms" and "go ons," that I decide I just can't lie to him.

"Okay," I say. "He dropped in through the chimney."

"Don't touch it," he says.

"That's where you come in," I say, launching into my plan: together we catch the squirrel and then release him into the park.

The line is very quiet. "Hello?" I say. "Are you there?"

"I'll be truthful. If we catch the squirrel, we won't be releasing it."

I thank him for his help. What did I expect? He's an animal *controller*, not a rescuer. I don't ask him to describe the procedure. Lethal injection? A tiny gas chamber? My great-grandfather shot squirrels for food—my mother remembers eating squirrel stew and fried squirrel, which she describes as very tasty—and even sold the skins when times got hard.

The phone rings. It's my older sister from California, who calls at least once a week. Jennifer, like my other sisters, believes in things like fortune telling, homeopathic remedies, animal totems, Feng Shui. So when I tell her about the squirrel, I'm not surprised that she suggests that the universe may be trying to tell me something. "Sometimes animals come into our lives to call attention to some aspect of ourselves we're not taking care of." I listen, more than a bit skeptical. It's hard to embrace someone else's beliefs, even your own sister's. Still, it's hard to deny the way the squirrel literally dropped into our lives: a dramatic entrance, to say the least. I tell her, sure, go ahead and do some research. See what the books say. In the meantime, I've got more pressing matters. There's a real-life squirrel trapped on the ledge, and I need a plan.

Sunday, September 9

When I smell coffee brewing, I crawl out from under the covers. Leila jumps from the bed and follows me into the living room, where Donald is sitting in the middle of the floor with the cat carrier in front of him, slipping a piece of twine through the front latch. He's already dressed, and the *Sunday Times* is on the coffee table. "He's back," he says, motioning to the window. The squirrel is sitting on his haunches beside the large clay pot, his front paws lifted. The two plastic containers are knocked over, and there's no sign of the peanuts. Leila circles the cat carrier, sniffs, then runs to hide beneath the futon. She always hides when we bring out the carrier. I don't blame her; usually it means a cab trip across town to the vet's.

"A brilliant idea," I say after a few sips of coffee, when Donald's plan becomes clear to me: we put the carrier on the balcony, thread the twine through the window opening, and wait.

"Then, when he comes for the peanuts . . ." Donald says, jerking the twine. The door of the carrier slams shut. "The tough part will be latching it. If an animal's cornered, he's likely to bite. I'll put some gloves out."

"He's really quick," I say.

"We'll put the peanuts way back into the carrier, to buy us some time." Donald opens the window, which sends the squirrel scurrying to the railing. He sets the carrier on the balcony, sprinkling a handful of peanuts deep inside. Then he positions the carrier so that we can see through its gated door, and threads the twine back through the window.

I station myself on the floor by the window, my hand grasping the end of the twine. The squirrel lifts his head; his nose twitches. He's so close I can see his white chest pumping small, quick breaths. There's no visible wound on either paw, but it's hard to tell since both are curled up tightly. I stay as still as I can, barely blinking. The slightest movement and he'll be out of here.

Donald sits on the couch and starts reading the *Times*, beginning with the front page. I always go for the real estate section. It's my addiction. Even though I know it will be years before we'll ever be able to afford our own place, if even then, I can't seem to help myself. I fantasize about townhouses, duplexes, maisonettes, prewar and postwar apartments, every kind of dwelling except a high-rise. I like being close to the ground, to use the stairs instead of the elevator.

Donald finishes the front section and picks up one of the New York guidebooks we keep on the coffee table. "It's our day off," Donald says. "We can't stay here all day waiting for a damned squirrel." The "damned" is for my benefit, a kind of verbal bluster he puts on when he feels he's losing ground.

He's right, of course. We need to see the sights. Once I'm out and about in the city, I enjoy exploring the neighborhoods, museums, and galleries, but unless I'm coerced, I'm content to stay in the apartment or to visit the neighboring haunts I've come to think of as mine: the park, the Y, the Japanese florist, the Korean greengrocer, the Irish pub. "It's a beautiful day," he says. "How about this?" His finger is on a page marked City Island, a small town in the Bronx that the guidebook describes as a mariner's village reminiscent of turn-of-the-century Maine. They'll need to revise their description, I'm thinking, since we've recently turned another century. Things change—in a moment, in the twinkling of an eye. A First Nation tribe, the Naskapi, called themselves "the people from the place where things disappear," but lately I've been thinking that all places are places where things disappear. That's what Salgado was saying with his photographs.

The best way to get to City Island is by car, which will require an hour's bus ride into Queens, where we keep our twelve-year-old Toyota parked on a street outside our friends' apartment. It's too expensive to keep a car in Manhattan, but we like having a car close by in case we need to escape—for a weekend, a day, or permanently, if things don't work out with the sublet or with Donald's new job. We've not used the car as much as we originally thought we would. For the first few months I thought I couldn't possibly breathe on this, well, island. I hate thinking of Manhattan as an island. If I entertain that fact for more than a minute, I'm gripped with a physical pain, like a fist pounding the center of my chest. One of the best things about living in Midtown, with no view of the water, is that it's possible to go for days without remembering that you're marooned on a tiny strip of land with millions of other people, and that the only way out is through a few tunnels and bridges that, in the case of some catastrophe, would be grossly insufficient as escape routes. And the boats and ferries would fill up fast.

If push came to shove, I suppose you could swim. Roosevelt Island is close enough, but then you're back where you started from: an island, just a different one. There's no lack of islands near the city. Some are tiny, with strange-sounding names—Hog Island, Cat Briar Island, the Chimney Sweep Islands, Rat Island. Each day, part of the prison population from Riker's Island is ferried and then bussed to Hart Island, more commonly known as Potter's Field, where prisoners dig graves for the unidentified or unclaimed. The first person buried in Potter's Field was a young immigrant woman who was born at sea, was later orphaned, and died in a Manhattan hospital. Since then, there have been more than 750,000 burials. I'd like to go there just to see what it's like, to see how they mark, or don't mark, the anonymous graves.

Monday, September 10

I wake thinking about islands. I write in my journal *island, insular, isolation,* then throw on some shorts and a T-shirt and go to the bookshelf where I keep the twenty-volume *Oxford English Dictionary* Donald gave me for my fiftieth birthday last year. Yes, the words are connected, as I'd suspected. I scan the page, skimming over entries. Island of Reil? This is news to me, the name for the center of the cerebrum. Strange to think that a group of cells can float in the middle of other cells that are completely different in structure; even stranger that they can all coexist peaceably within the same body.

"Almost," Donald says, and I look up from my desk. He's dressed for work, kneeling beside the window with his hand on the twine. The gate on the carrier is shut.

"So the third time wasn't the charm after all," I say.

When we got back from City Island late yesterday, the pea-nuts were gone. We replaced them and kept watch for nearly an hour. The squirrel kept lifting his head from the pot, but he didn't budge. I watched from a distance, just barely out of what I estimated to be the squirrel's sight line, and when he scuttled into the carrier, I hurried to the window, but he was too quick. This morning, the squirrel's been bold-er, perching beside the gated door, even partially entering the carrier while we stand within inches of him on the oth-er side of the glass. Twice I reached for the twine, but the squirrel scampered out.

"That's it," Donald says as he heads for the door. "We're not a squirrel restaurant. Catch him by tomorrow, or we're calling the city."

After he leaves, I open the window and the carrier gate, repositioning the twine for the next attempt. Across the street, office lights start coming on, one at a time. A young woman enters a cubicle, switches on the fluorescent tube above her desk. She walks to the window, sips something from a cup, stares out toward the street. She has lovely hair, dark and heavy.

The phone rings. I stand up and walk to the desk. It's Jennifer again. "You're up early," I say. It's five thirty in Cal-ifornia.

"I couldn't sleep." She asks about the squirrel and I fill her in. "It's very possible that the squirrel may be your totem," she says.

Great, I think. Just what I need. A dirty, common, beady-eyed, nervous rodent. Why not a hawk, a tiger, a pea-cock? Something regal and wise, or at least beautiful. But I know enough about animal totems to know you don't choose them. They choose you.

"The squirrel is all about balance," she says. "Balance and preparedness."

"I'm already balanced," I say.

"Between aloneness and society," she continues. "Give and take. Squirrels aren't solitary creatures. They're sociable, playful."

"I'm playful," I snap. True, I suppose I could be more sociable. I used to be, back in North Carolina. I get tired more easily here. New York is a tiring city. You see it on the faces of people in the subway, on buses, in restaurants and diners. Even those of us who don't have to push carts, sleep on the streets, work twelve-hour shifts, live four to a room, or commute hours a day by bus or train look tired. There's just so much to take in. No wonder we seal ourselves off. "It's hard to know how much to save for yourself and how much to give away," I say.

"That's where preparedness comes in. The squirrel saves nuts for the winter."

"Exactly," I say. And we've done that, socked away enough for several cold winters. Plus we have our Toyota, our escape plan. "You can never be too prepared, is my motto."

"You can't prepare for everything." She's right, of course. It's impossible to prepare for the unexpected; that's why it's called the unexpected. "But squirrels are adaptable," she reminds me. "They survive. Believe me, there are worse totems."

◦◦◦

For the rest of the morning, I play hide-and-seek with my totem. I plant peanuts; he takes them. I reach for the twine; he runs. "Your hours are numbered," I say aloud, then catch myself. If I keep this up, pretty soon I'll be joining the squirrel lady on the bench beside the South Pond. There's a pigeon lady, too, and even a rat guy who hangs out at the shallow part of the pond. "You shouldn't encourage them," a man in a business suit yelled at him one day, but the guy just kept sprinkling the pretzel crumbs. Can a rat be a totem? I guess there's something for everyone out there.

In the afternoon, I return to my essay about Salgado, but I can't focus. It's a gorgeous day, and I'm itching to get to the park. Salgado would approve, I'm sure. When he's not taking photographs he's planting trees, trying to save the rain forests in his homeland. He may live in France now, but his heart is in Brazil. I fantasize for a moment about planting a tree on the balcony. Could it grow tall enough to confuse the sparrows that sometimes perch on the railing? Would they build a nest in its branches?

Now a horn is blaring down on the street, and other horns are joining in. What is it this time? I go to the window to investigate. A fancy sedan is stopped in the middle of the street, sideways, blocking the yellow cab behind it. A tall, well-dressed woman gets out of the sedan and marches over to the cab. She's fuming, screaming at the cab driver that she's just trying to park her car but he won't give her an inch, and how is she supposed to back into the space with him right behind her like that, blasting his horn? The cab driver, who looks Middle Eastern, jumps out of the cab and stands nose to nose with the woman, shouting something I can't make out. I'm thinking it might come to physical blows. "Go back where you came from!" she screams, and someone on the sidewalk below my window—I can't see who it is—applauds.

So much for my theory of paddleboats and islands. Go

back where you came from? What would that mean for New York? I imagine the streets emptying like they do when you show a film in reverse, time sucking us backwards, the sky filling with bodies, all of us hurtling back to where we came from: the cab driver back to Saudi Arabia or Pakistan; the super and his wife and children, linked in a chain of hands, flying out of the basement apartment and into the air above the Atlantic, heading toward Montenegro; the ashes of Donald's grandparents reconstructing into bones, skin, cells, then swirling back to Chicago, Canada, Switzerland, and finally into a small village outside St. Petersburg; all of us disappearing, even me, sucked through the streets of New York and down to North Carolina then South Carolina, to Maryland, California, then back into Virginia, Texas, Illinois, landing finally in Indiana, in the nursery of a small hospital in Tippecanoe County, my thumb in my mouth, and still the film keeps running backwards, a hundred years, another hundred years, another. Where are they now—the streets of New York, the town of the past, the land where things disappear? No more. All that's left is forest, river, sky, and a few hundred gray squirrels, high in the trees, building their lopsided nests.

Tuesday, September 11

Strange, the way things happen while you're busy doing something else. Donald is out the door, having left early to walk the twenty blocks down Fifth Avenue to work. It's a glorious, crisp morning, and I've opened the window to catch a breeze, but I'm in my writing uniform and my hair is standing on end, so I know there's no chance I'll be showing myself in public. Later, maybe, before animal control arrives with whatever contraption they'll arrive with, I'll tidy myself up, but for now I'm at the desk with Leila in my lap. Across the street, a light comes on in a cubicle, and the dark-haired woman walks to the window and looks out, holding a cup in her hand but not drinking, just staring out as if waiting for the morning, or her life, to begin.

Then I hear a rattle and glance toward the balcony. The squirrel is climbing into the carrier, his tail flicking side to side. On instinct I rise from the chair, spilling Leila onto the floor, and approach slowly from behind, in no hurry because I'm sure he'll outsmart me anyway. I lean toward the window, calmly reach for the twine, and pull. Easy as that. The gated door slams shut. I grasp the twine tightly with both hands, pull it taut, and hold. Then, my left hand still holding the twine, I reach with my right hand for the glove, bring it to my mouth, and, securing the glove with my teeth, wedge my hand inside. Leila is beside me, hissing, but there's nothing to do but open the window and reach for the latch. The squirrel is squeaking, squealing an unearthly cry, and now his teeth are on the metal grate, gnawing. I snap the latch. It holds.

I carry Leila into the bedroom and close the door. The squirrel is still squealing, a sound like nothing I've ever heard, and all I can think is I've got to get him out of here, back to where he came from. I slip into some tennis shoes, grab Donald's long-sleeved flannel shirt because it's probably cool outside, and with the way the squirrel is gnawing on that gate, I should cover up anyway; in fact, maybe I need a jacket, so I slip that on too. I throw an old towel over the carrier, head for the door, and hurry down five flights of stairs, holding the carrier away from my body, the squirrel squealing, banging against the side of the carrier.

I'm heading north up Sixth Avenue before I realize how crazy I must look, in shorts and tennis shoes and a jacket, an old flannel shirt hanging beneath it, carrying—what?— some wild thing, a bird maybe, screaming to be let out. A woman with two large dogs is coming toward me as I cross Fifty-Sixth Street, and the dogs begin straining against their leashes, but I hurry on, trying not to look into the faces of the young businessmen in their crisp, tailored suits, carrying their briefcases and glancing at me quickly, then looking away. Now another woman with a dog is approaching; he's growling at the carrier. The squirrel squeals back, and I keep going, crossing Fifty-Seventh, Fifty-Eighth, Fifty-Ninth.

My arm is throbbing. At the edge of the park I stop at a bench, beside a homeless guy with a shopping cart. "What you got there?" he says, but I don't answer. The squirrel is quiet now—no sound, no movement—and I think for a moment maybe the excitement has killed him, and isn't that just the way things happen? After all the trouble, the five days of stalking and worry, I'll end up burying him in the park. I lift the towel and peer inside. He's curled at the back of the carrier, still breathing. Maybe he smells the trees, the acorns. Maybe he senses something.

I pick up the carrier and walk down the path that curves beside the pond, past the skating rink and the carousel, looking up into the bluest sky I've ever seen, searching for the highest tree. I find it: a huge oak among other huge oaks, surrounded by several large, smooth rocks. On one, a man is stretched out, the sun streaming over his leathery face. He raises up on one arm and watches me for a while, then puts his head back down.

I set the carrier down at the base of the oak, take off the jacket and spread it on the ground, still damp with dew. I lean back on my elbows and look up. The tree is full and cartoon-green, sunlight flickering through the leaves. The air is crisp, clean. I breathe it in. Is this what morning feels like? I really should get out more. I turn onto my side and put my head down, close to the carrier, and look inside. The squirrel is still curled at the back. With one quick movement, I spring the latch. Welcome back, I think, and mean it so much that I say it aloud.

Nothing happens. The squirrel is silent. He doesn't budge. I gather some acorns and place them in front of the open gate. In the distance, a siren starts wailing, then another and another and another. There must be a big fire somewhere. I look up, but see no smoke, just green stretching in all directions, and the blue sky wedged, in small pieces, between the branches. The squirrel peeks out of the carrier, his head darting side to side, his whiskers twitching. He sniffs at the acorns, then darts out, scurrying toward the base of the tree. A few more flicks of the tail, and he's skittering up the trunk. Up, up, stopping at each branch to look down, as if he wants to tell me something. His tail quivers, his head bobs and then, in a moment, *in the twinkling of an eye*, he's gone. I watch until there's no sign of him anywhere, just a shiver in the highest branch, beside a patch of blue, blue sky.

Eighth Avenue Moment

A YOUNG MAN STUMBLES toward me, something dark and feathered bundled in his arms. He looks up—red eyes, distillery breath: "You know anything about pigeons?"

"No," I say.

"I love animals, the ones on the farm when I was young." He holds the pigeon out to me. "What's wrong with him?"

"Looks like he's dying," I say.

"Why?"

"Things die. I'm sorry."

"I love animals," he says.

"I'm sorry."

"I love you too," he says.

Tears, Silence, Song

> There are three aspects of mourning: with tears, that
> is the lowest; with silence, that is higher; with a song,
> that is the highest.
>
> —Hasidic saying

September 11, 2001
What I did today:
1. released a squirrel
2. made chocolate pudding
3. tried to give blood
4. tried to pray

Rereading the journal entry, what surprises is not the list itself, odd though my actions might seem given the entry's date. The squirrel had dropped through the chimney into our apartment four days before and then escaped out an open window to the Juliet balcony, where I'd finally captured it in the cat carrier on the morning of the attacks. I was releasing the squirrel in Central Park when the sirens began.

And I can explain the chocolate pudding, a treat I generally deny myself, but which seemed, on the scale of the morning's horror, hardly an evil act. A generous act, even, something a mother might offer to soothe a distraught child. So yes, I admit it, I doubled the recipe and ate most of the pudding warm, right out of the pan, standing at the fifth-floor window of our Midtown sublet and watching the stunned pedestrians who were watching the smoke-blackened sky, their cell phones pressed to their ears. Donald was home by then, visibly shaken, his office having emptied out shortly after the attacks.

Even the third item on the list doesn't surprise me. Within hours after the attacks, newscasters announced that thousands of New Yorkers had lined up to give blood. Blood! Of course! I remember thinking. Never mind that I have rolling veins and have twice been turned away at blood drives because I'm borderline anemic; my blood could save a life! As I grabbed my purse and headed for the door, I turned to say goodbye to Donald. He was slumped on the sofa, hands in his lap. His eyes were red-rimmed, his face pinched in pain. He shook his head. He must have sensed, as the firefighters and other first responders and eyewitnesses and even Red Cross workers surely knew by then: blood was not the answer. Had I stopped to consider this, that all the blood in Manhattan could not help at this point, I would not have jogged—like some Clark Kent morphing into Superman—the ten blocks across Fifth Avenue to the Eastside hospital where I was turned away at the door.

But had I stayed where I belonged and not ventured out, I would not have seen the open doors of one, two, three—count them, four—houses of worship. Though I belong to no church and rarely attend services, I often duck inside while making my daily round of errands to escape the heat, cold, or rain, or just to enjoy some quiet amid the screech of Midtown chaos. Catholic, Episcopal, Greek Orthodox cathedrals; Presbyterian, Pentecostal, Lutheran churches. Any open door will do. I was raised Southern Baptist, but, stifled by the doctrine, I left that fold in my late teens and never looked back.

But oh, how I miss the music. Sometimes, walking on a side street—in West Harlem, Midtown, the East Village—I'll pass a storefront church and hear a choir practicing a familiar hymn, and I'll slip into a back pew. If no one else is around, I'll close my eyes and sing along, imagining the soprano line scrolling across the page, the alto and tenor lifting in and out of the space between the clefts, and the bass line fastening me to the present moment. I studied voice in college, paying my tuition by singing solos for weddings and funerals, but it was the choral music I lived for, the cantatas and oratorios, the feeling of standing in the center of all that sound, my voice no longer mine alone but rather a single strand woven into the tapestry: one breath, one voice.

The open church door I entered the day of the attacks was a Catholic cathedral. Which may account for #4 of the journal entry. Notice I didn't write "prayed" but rather "tried to pray." Beyond the fact that I was out of practice, years out of practice, there was the matter of the kneeling benches. Kneeling always makes me feel like a fraud, someone playing the part of a believer.

Not that I'm ungrateful for the presence of kneeling benches. I'm grateful for all the furnishings and rituals that were missing from my Baptist childhood: flickering votives, prayer cards, stained glass, dizzying incense, carved crucifixes, the font of holy water, the sprinkling of Latin phrases, all that mystery. In the Baptist church of my childhood there was no pomp, little circumstance, and even less mystery, though one December our youth choir director tried to infuse some into our Christmas cantata. I'd been assigned the soprano solo: doloroso, the director called it. "There are no words," he said. "It's a lament."

I'd never heard of such a thing. Wasn't singing all about words? He showed me the passage from the book of Jeremiah that he would read to the congregation while I sang: "In Rama was there a voice heard, lamentation, and weeping, and great mourning, Rachel weeping for her children, and would not be comforted, because they are not."

"Are not?" I asked. "What does that mean?"

He said he wasn't sure but that he thought it meant her children were dead, or she was crying for an end to the suffering of all children or maybe just the children of Israel. "The important thing to remember," he said, "is that it is doloroso. Rachel is mourning. She is in pain. Don't make it pretty."

⌘

As I entered the cathedral that afternoon, I lit a votive and took a seat on a pew near the back. The cathedral was eerily quiet except for the creak of wooden pews and an occasional sniffle or sigh. All around me, people were kneeling. Some fingered rosaries, their lips moving silently, their heads bowed or gazing up toward the stained glass windows. What were they saying, praying? What words, and in what tongue? The man kneeling beside me was weeping unashamedly, tears dropping onto an open prayer book. Did he know someone at the Trade Center? A brother, sister, someone gone missing? I made a prayer steeple with my hands, pressing them together the way Sunday School teachers had taught me. Dear Lord, I began in my head, waiting for something to rise up, some script to follow.

"Tried to pray," I had written. But even that entry does not surprise me, nor, I trust, does it indict me. "In prayer it is better to have a heart without words than words without a heart," wrote John Bunyan. No, what surprises me about my 9/11 list is not that I was unable to pray. What surprises is what is missing: tears. The lowest form of grief, according to the Hasidic saying. Never mind the higher rungs—silence, song—I could not even reach the lowest.

∽

We woke the next morning to an acrid smell, like electrical wires burning. I could taste it on my tongue. The Trade Center is three or four miles from us, I thought. Can smoke travel that far? Donald was already up, grinding the coffee beans as he does each morning. Morning coffee is a ritual, something I count on and which he knows I count on. No matter what has transpired the day before, there is always the music of the coffee grinder. That morning, I lay in bed longer than usual, stroking the cat's back, and when I heard a ripping sound I went into the living room, where Donald stood at the window holding a roll of duct tape.

"We need to seal up the windows," he said. "The fireplace too." He explained about the smell—yes, he agreed, electrical wiring. But also burned plastic and metal, soot, and dust particles. The fires would smolder for days, he guessed, and each time the wind shifted, the smell would sift our way.

The *New York Times* was on the table: "U.S. Attacked" was the headline, with a photo of the Twin Towers engulfed in red flames and black smoke. I walked to the window and looked down at the empty street. Well, almost empty. There, on the sidewalk in front of Au Bon Pain, was the homeless man who stops each morning to rummage through the clear plastic bag of day-old bakery goods placed on the sidewalk the evening before. He always removes a bagel. Just one. I admire that about him. He might be picky, but he isn't greedy.

That morning, though, the sidewalk was empty: no plastic bag. The man stood there a long time, looking lost, unmoored. He adjusted his backpack and glanced up, as if expecting his morning bagel to fall from the sky, a sky that was almost as blue as it had been the morning before. Watching him, I felt a stinging at the edges of my eyes and was seized by an impulse to open the sealed window and call down to him, but what would I say? What could I offer?

Once Donald had finished sealing up the fireplace opening, we sat at the table and drank our coffee. We stared at the front page of the *Times*. We ate our yogurt and fruit. Donald's office, like most of the offices in New York, was closed. We had the whole day before us. It was a beautiful, sunlit day. Still, like hundreds of thousands of other Americans that morning, we did not venture out. We turned on the television, which belonged to our landlords, as did almost everything in our furnished sublet. We sat side by side on our landlords' worn, lumpy sofa and watched the networks repeat the images all morning long—the towers aflame, then falling. Again. And again.

I don't remember much of what we did the rest of the day, probably because we did nothing much. I remember walking to the grocery store through ghostly quiet streets, standing in a silent line at the meat counter trying to decide what to buy or if I wanted to buy anything. I remember returning phone calls to my parents in Indiana and my siblings in California and North Carolina. At one point, Rob and Amy called. Two decades younger than we are, the Roys are our closest New York friends and have become our surrogate family, especially since the birth of their daughter.

Rob and I are both freelancers, so our schedules are more flexible than Donald's and Amy's. I helped Rob paint their kitchen and nursery a few weeks before Marcella was born, and I sometimes babysit during the day, as I babysat for all fifteen of my nephews and nieces. Marcella loves patty-cake and nursery rhymes, and I've recently started singing songs for her while she nods in rhythm or makes the motions with her hands—"The Wheels on the Bus," "Old MacDonald," and her new favorite, "The Itsy Bitsy Spider."

I believe Rob and Amy sense that I need Marcella more than she needs me, which makes their ordinary gesture that day—of calling to check on us, of putting Marcella close to the speakerphone so we could hear her—an extraordinary one. The child's words were not the point. It was the lilt of her toddler babble, the song of someone who knew nothing of the attacks, whose whole world was Mama, Dada, cookie, milk, my, go, bye-bye. Rob mentioned that he planned to take Marcella to the park in a day or two and maybe I'd like to come along.

∝∞∾

Two nights after the attacks, the rains began, waking me from a fitful sleep. Rain batted against our sealed bedroom window, pinging on the window air conditioner where pigeons often roost. I lay beside Donald, my hand on his chest riding its rise and fall, trying to match my breath to his so I could sleep. Two a.m., three a.m., four, Donald's chest falling and lifting. No rest for the diggers, I thought, with their headlamps and shovels, the rain pouring onto their helmets, their drenched jackets, into their buckets, into their boots as they sloshed through the wreckage, rain filling the holes as fast as they could dig them. My mind tunneled back through the last few days—news reports, body counts, hundreds of "have you seen" flyers with Xeroxed faces of those gone missing, flyers now blown against fences and sodden with rain, and what about the dogs, the Life Dogs and Death Dogs, had the rain washed away the scents they tracked?

As I lay in the dark, my father's face floated to me—a six-year-old memory—his face contorted with pain as he shook his head side to side, his voice keening. We were at my parents' home in Indiana. We'd buried his younger brother just hours before, across the border in Illinois. A storm had gathered as we drove east into Indiana and had not let up. At my parents' kitchen table, I watched my father's shoulders lift and fall, lift and fall, his hands pressing hard against his face. Rain was slapping against the kitchen window. He moved his hands from his face and looked directly into my eyes. "It's raining," my father kept saying, "on all those graves." His face was wet with tears that would not stop.

⁓

By the third morning after the attacks, the city began to wake—Midtown offices, restaurants, corner bodegas, newsstands. Yet everything and everyone seemed to be moving in slow motion, keeping a respectful distance. It was still raining. Sounds were muted. Yellow cabs again appeared on the streets, but few horns blared, and when they did, they seemed to lack conviction, as if drivers were apologizing for breaking the silence.

Donald's office had reopened, and after he left for work I was struck by the stillness that filled the apartment. The loud, percussive assault I'd come to expect from our neighbors over the past few years—the boot-stomping, door-slamming, furniture-scraping, toilet-flushing soundtrack of a Midtown apartment house—was missing. If the noisy neighbors above us were home, they must have removed their cleated boots. Maybe they were tiptoeing across the floor in stockinged feet this very moment, wondering why their neighbor below wasn't clanging pans in the kitchen or cursing the computer that had once again frozen up right in the middle of a paragraph that might break open the whole essay, the paragraph that was now lost, frozen somewhere in cyberspace, irretrievable. If so, if they were listening for the accustomed curses of their downstairs neighbor struggling to put words on the page, they needn't have worried. Their downstairs neighbor, as it turned out, had no words.

But maybe, I thought, maybe on this National Day of Prayer and Remembrance, someone did. I turned on the television. It was raining in DC as well, umbrellas of every color floating across the screen toward the National Cathedral. The Navy Sea Chanters sang and then the Boy and Girl Choristers, their young faces like flowers opening. Soon a brown face appeared at the lectern, a thoughtful-looking man with large, thick glasses. He began to read from Jeremiah ("Rachel weeping for her children, and would not be comforted . . .") and I half expected a mournful keen to rise up, but only his words issued forth, and then it was the camera's turn, panning across the profiles of presidents: the two Bushes, Clinton, Ford, and Carter, their heads in varying shades of gray and white. They looked so old, so weary, that I had to turn away from the television, toward the window. Rain and more rain.

Music brought me back to the screen. A bearded man was seated on a chair, cradling—I know no other word for it—a guitar, and as he plucked he rocked forward, then back, then forward, the movement so subtle that those seated in the cathedral could not have seen it, but the video camera bridged the distance. I watched the rocking and his small, ordinary hands and his eyes glancing up at the tall, stately woman standing beside him. I recognized her from opera broadcasts, Denyce something. But I could not call her last name until it appeared on the screen: Graves. Of course, I thought, and what a dark name to bear all your life. But if anyone could bear it, this beautiful woman could. Her black dress swept the floor. Black, black, and more black, which made the gardenia corsage pinned to the bodice stand out in white relief.

Even if I'd muted the sound, her face would have been enough. The broad face haloed by dark hair, the smooth brown plane of her forehead, the high cheekbones, the eyebrows lifted in, what? Pain? Surprise? Sudden recognition? Something had entered her, and she was absorbing it even as we watched. She was absorbing it, taking it in as hers alone, and giving it back to us as ours.

My throat tightened with each phrase—"alabaster cities gleam, undimmed by human tears"—yet even those words did not break me. Then, as the camera shifted from her face to the rows of aging men seated together, something shifted inside me, inside them. I read it in their faces. The gray- and white-haired men, leaders who swore that even in the middle hour of our grief they would rid the world of evil, were in that moment not Bush, Bush, Clinton, Ford, and Carter. They were George, George, Bill, Gerald, and Jimmy, a row of boys swallowing the pain and wincing at the tears forming in their eyes, two of the boys actually mouthing the words, and as she sang I could almost hear their mothers calling—*it's getting dark, time to come in now*—and my mother calling to me and my voice answering. For in the middle hour of our grief we are always and only children. Thus it has always been and thus it will always be, and that is why Rachel was weeping.

⁓⤸

By the time Donald arrived home from work my eyes were swollen, my throat raw. He sat beside me on the sofa. "Let's go look at our city," he said. I wondered if he was thinking of the scene in *The World According to Garp*, when the husband, suffering a crisis, asks his wife to go with him to their children's room to watch them sleep: "Let's go look at the children," the husband says. Our city was sleeping, for this moment anyway. Yes, I thought, we should go look at it.

Once we were out on the street, I saw I didn't need the umbrella. The rain had finally stopped. Next door, a worker from Au Bon Pain was carrying a clear plastic bag out to the sidewalk, larger than the bags the bakery usually set out. The bag was filled with bagels, muffins, baguettes, croissants. Day-old? Perhaps. But maybe they'd been baked that very day, the bakers preparing more than necessary, and why not? All over the city, chefs and bakers were working round the clock to feed workers, victims' family members, whoever needed to be fed. The worker took a small knife from his pocket and sliced an opening at the top of the bag. Just large enough for a hand to reach inside. An open invitation.

We walked south on Sixth Avenue, officially named Avenue of the Americas but it's always been Sixth to me. I take it whenever I can, anything to avoid the noise and the snarl of foot traffic on Broadway. But after a few blocks, Donald took my hand and guided me west toward Broadway. American flags covered the windows of apartment buildings, hotels, and storefronts; they waved from fire escapes and scaffolding. Police officers were stationed at every corner and doorway, but Donald and I met only two or three approaching pedestrians, all of whom stepped aside politely to give us room. The usual neon billboards flashed across the screens above Times Square, but the small crowd gathered in the triangle seemed more intent on the sepia-toned image on the bottom screen: a live feed of Ground Zero. The vast landscape of dirt, debris, and twisted metal seemed otherworldly, a gray, apocalyptic nightmare whose only signs of life were the workers in their bright helmets, looking, from this distance, like tiny toy figures a child could grasp with one hand.

At Forty-Second Street we turned east, walking silently past Bryant Park to Fifth Avenue. I needed to see the library lions, and there they were, Patience and Fortitude, their marble countenances unchanged. Had they turned their heads to look south, they would have seen gray plumes of smoke rising into the sky. Donald and I sat for a few moments on the library steps, then turned north to head back home. More police officers, more flags, more handmade signs. The display windows of Saks, draped in black, were empty except for an American flag placed every four or five windows, each with a spray of flowers beneath it and the words "With Sadness."

At Rockefeller Plaza, where in winter ice skaters gather, a gilded Prometheus flew above empty tables, his right hand grasping a cluster of fire. "The fire that hath proven to mortals a means to mighty ends," if we trust the translator of Aeschylus whose words float above the sculpture.

Prometheus, stealing fire from the gods so that we mortals can paint, sculpt, write poems, make music, design buildings that can scrape the heavens and burst into flame. No wonder the gods punished him.

And here, rising above Prometheus, seventy stories high, was another building aiming at the heavens. If it too burst into flame, would it be punishment from the gods, or an act of purification? The "purifying fire of sacrifice," to borrow John D. Rockefeller's words. In three years of living in the city, Donald and I had never paused to study the plaque listing Rockefeller's core principles, but now we did: "Only in the purifying fire of sacrifice is the dross of selfishness consumed and the greatness of the human soul set free." Is sacrifice the only way to escape ourselves, then? To become part of something greater? Given the silence of that evening, the empty streets, the pillars of smoke rising in the downtown sky, to elevate human sacrifice seemed obscene, incomprehensible. If someone or something greater was in charge, I hoped for Rockefeller's "all-wise and all-loving God, named by whatever name."

As we walked the last few blocks, the Avenue of the Americas was so quiet I was certain I heard a traffic light change. Donald took the apartment keys from his pocket; we were almost home. In front of Au Bon Pain, the homeless guy was back, bending down on one knee, his hand inside the bakery bag. He removed his usual bagel. No, two. Then he reached in deeper and pulled out a muffin, which he studied carefully, turning it in his hands. A huge muffin—I was hoping it was blueberry. Perfectly browned, with a substantial, crusty top dusted with sugar. Go ahead, I wanted to tell the man. Take two, take three. The crust will break open with the first bite, and just when you think it can't get any better, any softer or sweeter, a blueberry will burst forth and then another. You won't believe how good they are.

~∞~

Nearly a week past the attacks, recovery efforts at Ground Zero were still underway and would be for months to come. Hundreds of engineers, welders, ironworkers, and volunteers worked round the clock. Rescue workers sifted through wreckage amid the odor of smoke and decaying human remains. Dazed, exhausted family members still posted "have you seen" flyers. In Midtown, it was as if someone had clicked the restart button and turned off the mute. Cabs again filled the avenues. Pedestrians ventured out.

On Monday morning, after Donald left for work, I dressed for the park. A few minutes later, Rob appeared at the door, wearing his New York Yankees ball cap. Marcella was strapped into her stroller, kicking her legs back and forth. She'd been walking for a few months now and was obviously anxious to escape the stroller and light out on her own.

We crossed Fifty-Seventh and entered the park near the South Pond. The day was excruciatingly beautiful. It didn't seem right, it didn't seem just, for the weather to be so perfect. The park wasn't as crowded as usual, but those who were out were really out. Professional dog walkers with their fanny pouches and tangled leashes. Women jogging with strollers, some with post-partum bellies displayed between halter tops and shorts. Serious athletes running two by two, strutting their pecs, abs, delts, all those shortcut terms, moving as if there were mirrors all around them. Their vanity cheered me. As did the balloon hat on the juggler outside the entrance to the Central Park Zoo. I thought of the John Lahr quote: "Frivolity is the species' refusal to suffer."

A large rat scurried across the path—some things never change. Was my squirrel still around here? While Rob and Marcella watched the juggler, I hiked to the large rock overlooking the ball fields, stopping at the stand of trees where I'd released the squirrel from the cat carrier on the morning of the attacks. No sign of him. Well, of course no sign of him. Even if the squirrel was still there, having made these particular trees his own, how could I possibly recognize him? I wasn't thinking straight.

Our destination was the Adventure Playground. Not my favorite Central Park haunt, but kids seem to love it—the climbing pyramid, especially, and the central water channel and large sand pile. As we approached the playground, the first thing I saw was a small American flag. I'd never noticed a flag before, had it always been there? It stood at the edge of the sand pile and was lowered to half-staff, children playing noisily around it.

Rob was the only man present. One woman wore a headscarf and loose trousers; she was watching a small blond boy who was digging with a shovel in the sand. Rob lifted Marcella from her stroller and I took her hand, leading her toward the pyramid. She half-hopped, half-danced her way toward it, then suddenly broke free of my hand and turned toward the park benches. I followed close behind her until we reached the benches. She looked up at me and raised both arms, her signal for me to pick her up.

I sat on the bench and pulled her onto my lap, turning her to face the other children. Her head was sweaty, her brown hair curling at the nape of her neck. I breathed in her scent. She leaned her head against me. Several children were now at the sand pile, playing beneath the flag. The blond boy was intent on his digging. As he dug, he held up each treasure for the woman to see: a leaf, another leaf, a twig— and what was that bright red thing? A balloon? Yes, a scrap of a balloon! He held it out proudly, and as he brought it to his mouth I started to call out to Rob—but no need, for suddenly the woman was there. The moment opened in slow-motion, miniaturized beauty: a flag flying at half-staff, a pile of sand, and a woman in a headscarf, running her heart out to reach a blond boy.

Marcella's head began to bob in rhythm. She wanted a song. Her hands were busy, her fingers weaving, wiggling. She wanted the spider song, starring the itsy bitsy hero who won't take rain, won't take no for an answer. I placed my hands in front of hers to show her how to make him climb, up, up, up. I hadn't sung in a long time and my voice was rusty, but her bobbing head told me she needed the words, so the itsy bitsy spider went up the spout again.

Imagine

CROSSING STRAWBERRY FIELDS NEAR the dark-storied Dakota, I hear the wheels before I see them: two skate-boarders, heading downhill on a loop Yoko imagined decades ago—a Mohawked, tattooed white boy and behind him a skinny black boy with a dyed red ponytail.

"Watch out!" the black boy cries out to a stroller-pushing mom, who looks up but not in time, so he takes the hit for her, airborne for an instant, and then a cracking splat as he lands face down.

"Ooooh," onlookers exhale in unison.

The boy recovers quickly, springing up on his feet, blood dripping down his face. "Cool. That was awesome, man. I needed that," he says too loudly, looking up as if expecting praise from his friend. But Mohawk is long gone, having never even slowed, so little did his friend's moment register with him. The wounded boy retrieves his skateboard and climbs aboard, pushing off with one foot. "I'm fuckin' blee-din', man," he yells, breaking into a high-pitched laugh, a swipe of pride crossing his face.

As usual, a crowd of Lennon fans is gathered around the Imagine mosaic, but today the fans must navigate an encircling fence, peering around it and above to glimpse what they've journeyed to see. Some hold deli-wrapped bouquets; one woman grasps a candle.

"He's buried here?" a baseball-capped girl asks her father. "Right here, in the park?"

The father shakes his head no. "It's just a memorial. From a song."

Having now lived in New York long enough to insinuate my way through a crowd, I move closer to see what's going on inside the fence. Two workmen are kneeling, trowels in hand, a bucket of mortar between them. One wears a large crucifix around his neck; his khaki-covered knee obscures the mosaic's "I" and "M".

A dark-haired woman edges close. "Excuse me," she says, tapping him on the shoulder. "Excuse me," she repeats. "We are Brazil." She gestures to a bevy of young, dark-haired women, each lovelier than the next. "Can you please . . ." and she motions to the mosaic. The workman nods, and moves his knee aside.

Imagine retiling *Imagine*. But of course, everything requires maintenance. By the end of the day the broken stones will be repaired, the mosaic made whole once more, swept and polished by hands I now notice are rough and freckled. What is the man's story? A simple gold wedding band, fastened to his ring finger, is flecked with dried mortar. Perhaps in a few hours, after boarding the uptown A train and transferring to the D, the man will make his way up a third-floor walkup, nod to his sons bent over their homework, kiss the back of his wife's neck before crossing the room to the kitchen sink to scrub the ring clean with a brush she has placed for that purpose, and sit down to the dinner spread for him.

But this is *my* story, the one I need. The workman must

compose his own. And sing it, if he chooses, harmonizing with someone else or "all by his lonesome," as my grandmother used to say. The lone violinist at Bethesda Terrace, who plays for loose change, must arrive early to claim the choicest spot: the tunnel, where a hollowed-out emptiness enlarges the song.

Present Tense

THE DICTIONARY IS OPEN on my desk: *squirrel*. From the Greek, *skiouros*. Shadow-tail. What tails us when our back is turned. All morning I've been counting backwards in my mind, the years collapsing. Next week is our twenty-fifth wedding anniversary. How have we made it this far?

A car alarm whoops on the street below, and I swivel in my chair to look through the French doors that open into the living room. Some of the panes are original, but several have been replaced. On their last visit from the West Coast to check on their apartment, our landlords, a forty-something married couple, accidentally let the story slip out—something about a slammed door—and I thought, It takes some force to knock that many panes loose. Then I remembered what a mutual acquaintance had told us, something about an affair, long ago, and how the couple had weathered the crisis and reconciled. "Like a lot of people do," the friend had said, and I'd nodded casually, as if an affair were an abstract, theoretical matter, something that could never touch me.

When we first moved to New York, I expected that the energy of the streets, its pulsing beat, would drill me into the moment, render me Present Tense. Present. Tense. Why, then, sitting at my desk or walking the streets, am I more past then present? More tensile than tense? Yesterday as I was walking in the Garment District, turning the corner of Thirty-Sixth and Sixth, the moment opened up, wide and deep. Opened *me* up, and suddenly there she was, my dead grandmother in her chiffon scarf peering into a window filled with buttons and plunging me forty years down the well of memory—her Indiana farmhouse, the button jar gleaming, my uncle with his muscled arms leaning forward on the table—and then, four blocks later and three flights down subway steps and in through the wheezing doors, I saw him again, my uncle, dead now twenty years, clasping the subway strap with one meaty hand, the other holding a folded *New York Times*, where the face of a young woman stared back at me. What is my photo doing there? I thought, until I was snapped back into the moment, my present-tense self in charge once again.

Of course it was not my photo. I am not a young woman. I am a middle-aged, long-married woman who spends her mornings with the *Oxford English Dictionary*, looking up words like *squirrel*. Yesterday I unpacked one of the boxes we'd brought with us when we moved into this furnished sublet. We'd stored it on a high shelf, behind our landlord's toolboxes, and I'd forgotten about it until I went looking for a hammer to finally hang the etching that had been leaning against the wall for months. Standing on the ladder to reach the toolbox, I saw the large lettering on the box: "Mementos." The box was heavy, but I managed to get it down to the floor, where I sliced the tape with an X-ACTO blade. Inside were our high school yearbooks, some old photos and playbills, Donald's Army medals and insignia, a stack of our love letters, and, at the bottom of the box, folded between two college textbooks, a small, flesh-colored hand towel. My chest tightened, my breath caught. I closed the box quickly, climbed back up the ladder, and pushed the box back as far as it would go.

❧

"Getting at the truth," we say, but why say it that way if truth is so obvious, so easy to uncover? Layer upon layer has grown over it. This has taken years. What is truth hiding from? And why is it so difficult to find its soft center? Sometimes to get at the truth, you must poke it with something sharp—a stick, a memory—until the stories spill out, each with its own lexicon.

Donald's story, for one. A story he never told his first wife, the young woman who gave birth to his son while awaiting his overseas return—from Korea, not Vietnam, for the universe had blessed him in that regard. But a story he did tell me, his second wife, who carried into our marriage the burden of my own stateside sins.

"What was it like over there?" I would ask again and again. And "Did you ever? Most soldiers did, right? Even the married ones."

Finally one night Donald answered. "The girls were everywhere. Girls in every bar, on every stool."

"Women," I corrected him.

He shook his head. "Girls," he said sadly. "Girls with babies. At first we didn't know about the babies. Or pretended we didn't know. You'd have a few drinks, it had been months since you'd seen your wife. The girls sat on the stools, twirling their straws in their drinks. They wore skirts slit up to here."

But already my mind was swinging away from his words and into the scene itself. How easy it was to imagine what he saw: down the length of the bar, a row of young Korean women in various outfits studied from American television. The one in hot pants and white go-go boots is the first to be claimed, and within minutes several soldiers have joined the other women, leaning into their faces, lighting cigarettes and ordering drinks. "You know the kind," Donald was saying. "The kind young girls like. Fruity, in tall glasses."

I could see the pastel drinks, the kind of drinks I ordered that dismal year after my first marriage ended. Drinks with paper umbrellas floating on top, maraschino cherries and orange slices speared onto miniature plastic swords, and with no effort at all I was inside Donald's memory, inside his skin as he watched the girls, their small, well-muscled thighs, one leg crossed over a knee, swinging a seductive circle. He was trying to get the courage to walk over to the girls, but their voices were loud and shrill. Inside the memory, my own head began to pound.

Then I saw her in my mind as he must have seen her: a small Korean woman dressed in a pink flowered dress and staring shyly into a pale drink, her feet crossed demurely at the ankles. She is using the swizzle stick as a straw, and when she looks up from her drink, she smiles. Her teeth are too big for her mouth, and she puts her hand over her mouth as if suddenly ashamed.

"The worst part," Donald was saying, "was afterwards, in her room. She had a child. That's what I can't get out of my mind."

But I wasn't ready to enter that part of the story; my mind was still in the smoky bar. The bartender was lowering the shades on the street window, on my own broken year alone, so many years ago. Lowering the shades of the bar where I met the man, where began the months of ruin, and how could I let that happen, the man had a wife, he had children—dear God, what was I thinking?

"Maybe your money bought her child a good breakfast," I said to Donald. I wanted to comfort him, to find reasons around the truth. The truth is, it was all too easy to slip back into his story, following the girl stumbling in her cheap American-style shoes down the crooked street, through the alley, into the tiny room.

The man I met in the bar had a wife and two children he went home to every evening and whom he swore he would never leave no matter how much he loved me. The year before Donald appeared in my life, my loneliness was mute, wordless, feral. At night I would park my car near the man's house, look in at the yellow lamps in the window, watch his lovely wife float through the dining room, her arms loaded with a dinner platter, and behind her the young daughter and then the man carrying a son on his back, and when he reached the table he slid the boy into the high chair and leaned down to kiss his neck.

During those months and for years later, even after Donald and I had married, I dreamed of cupboards and cubbyholes, me hiding inside them, shrunken into some tiny version of myself, Tinkerbell alighting on the surfaces where the wife's hands had rested. Sometimes her dream hand would reach into the cupboard where I was hiding—she was dusting, perhaps, or reaching for clean linens to spread onto the dinner table—and I would stare at the shiny ring on her finger. A wedding ring bigger than I was, I thought. Than I would ever be.

⁓

Who can trace the pattern of a marriage, its sinuous turns? You wake one day and realize that months have gone by, years, since you last looked across the table at your husband. Maybe you'd never looked. One night thirteen years into our marriage, I looked across the dinner table and saw that Donald was weeping. Earlier that day, we'd received word that his high school acting teacher, the elderly woman who thirty years before had taught him the King's English—how to plump up his vowels and bite consonants in two—had died. Now his eyes were filling, tears falling past his folded arms and onto the lace tablecloth. "I didn't realize," he kept saying. "I didn't know what she gave me. I should have thanked her."

Thirteen years into the marriage, and this was the first time I had seen Donald's tears, heard his voice breaking with a husky, adolescent catch. He was weeping for his teacher, yes, but the quality of the tears told me his grief went deeper. Something else was dying here, something that had nothing to do with his teacher. Something about the two of us. I looked across the table, the table that now seemed too wide. Whole continents divided us. Hidden topographies. All those places we had not traveled together. Things had to change.

But it was too late. That is what his tears were telling me. Glacial distances had opened, continental drift. The Other Woman had already come between us. No. Let me tell the truth now. *We* had come between us; the woman just happened to be there, waiting. As I had been there, waiting, all those years ago. Or so I had told myself. Had the man been happily married, I reasoned, he would not have noticed me to begin with.

Months after Donald had moved out to be with her, I

screamed into the phone, into the ear of the Other Woman. "What kind of woman are you? What kind of woman would break up a marriage?" I screamed until my throat was raw, but I was just getting started. "How could you do this? What kind of woman would do such a thing?"

When I finally stopped to grab a breath for the next onslaught, I heard the silence. A dramatic silence. The length and weight of a breath, a heartbeat. Hers? Mine?

When the silence broke, the voice was softer than I'd imagined it would be. "I once thought I could never do it either," the voice said. Another breath, another heartbeat. "It happened to me too, with my husband," the voice said. "It almost broke my heart."

How dare you, I thought after I'd slammed down the phone. How dare you ask for my sympathy.

⌐∞⌐

Books tell us it takes about six months for the initial passion of an affair to cool. It took the man with the children a little more than six months; Donald, a bit less. When I answered the door, I almost didn't recognize my own husband. He looked younger, smaller, his arms more delicate, vulnerable. For long minutes we sat like strangers, side by side on the sofa where we had once sprawled together reading the *New York Times* or watching a favorite movie. Exhausted from weeks of phone calls and letters and tentative moves toward each other, we had no more to say. But in those interminable minutes on the sofa—as we would learn months later, when we were finally able to open the silence—each of us, without consulting the other, decided that if we were to start over, it would have to be in a new place. A new start in a new home.

We got into his car—I remember he opened the door for me—and drove to a restaurant, then to his apartment, the temporary nest he had made. For himself, I would come to understand, for he had never had a place of his own before. Like me, Donald had gone directly from his parents' home into his first marriage and then, swiftly, into his second.

But this did not mean that the Other Woman had not been here in his nest, had not left her scent, which I must have taken in. How could I not have taken it in? I walked around the apartment, surprised at the sparseness. Wall-to-wall carpeting. Some generic pieces of rented furniture. A few pots and pans. Four cups and four plates. A chess set programmed for a single player. And in the bedroom, a bed into which the two of us fell.

A few days later, when I told my mother over the phone what had happened, that I had visited the apartment, had stayed the night, and in the morning made breakfast using the dishes and pans, she was silent. Then she sighed heavily. "I would have thrown it all out," she said. "Every cup and saucer."

I did not tell her I had also used the sheets and towels, and the bath mat the Other Woman's feet had touched. I knew what she would say, what any self-respecting wife would say. To this day, my actions make no sense. On one hand, I insisted that we buy a new home, for a new start. Yet when the day came to sort through the things that had padded his nest—Donald had offered to do this job himself—I said, "No, I'll do it."

So, on the morning before the move to the new home, I drove across town and made the turn into the apartment complex, counting the entrances to be sure I had located Building C, since all the buildings looked alike. I parked the car and walked past a row of identical doors, behind which who knew what lives were being lived? I took the key from my pocket and stood for a moment before the door, waiting. For what? For some nice woman to answer? A woman with two children, perhaps, who would invite me in for a glass of wine, sit beside me, and tell the stories of her life and loves, all those mysteries I had not as yet, and may never, solve.

When no one answered—of course no one answered—I turned the key in the lock and opened the door to the apartment, now emptied of furniture. Sunlight poured through the bare windows onto a small stack of dishes and linens beside a large packing box. I sat on the floor and carefully wrapped the cups and saucers, one by one, in white tissue paper and placed them into the box. I reached for the sheets, which were smoothed and freshly creased, their edges neatly squared. They looked good as new. Perfectly good. It would be a shame to throw them out. Or the towels, for that matter—the pale, flesh-colored bath and hand towels. Certainly there were many more years of use in them.

I placed everything in the box and carried it to my car, then drove to the Salvation Army store where a round, friendly man happily relieved me of everything.

No, not everything. At the last minute, I opened the box and pulled out one hand towel, then drove to the new house where I had already unpacked most of our household things. I folded the towel into a box, along with some old books and mementos, and placed the box in the deepest part of the storage closet. No one need ever know it was there.

That was twelve years ago. Twelve years since the thirteenth-year breakup and reconciliation. The lexicon of stories like ours is shaped from *re-* words: *reconciliation, repairing, restoring, redeeming.* All those words people employ in their search to understand what happened and why. Twelve plus thirteen equals twenty-five. Twenty-five years of marriage, come next week. I wonder if the man and his wife lasted this long, and if their children now have children of their own. I wonder if the box of mementos will follow us to our next home, and our next, or whether at some point we will let it go—to be discovered by someone whose job it is to sift through the belongings of strangers and decide what to toss, what to salvage, and where to store what remains.

Shirley, Goodness, and Mercy

The Kiss

A FEW MINUTES BEFORE the phone began ringing in our apartment, I was on a three-mile jog in Central Park carrying in my head a poem about kangaroos that I had begun writing a week before, shortly after returning from what I jokingly called the Routine Procedure. If you are anywhere near my age, you are familiar with the Routine Procedure—that unpleasant, potentially demeaning event every conscientious internist urges you toward as you approach your fiftieth birthday. I'd put it off for two years and had finally run out of excuses.

The procedure had gone well, and though the gastroenterologist had explained afterward—in his musical, resonant baritone—that he had "found something," he'd softened the news by saying that there was no reason to think the worst but that I should call his office the following Monday for the biopsy results.

Which is what I'd been planning to do when I got back from jogging that morning, but as I entered the apartment, the phone was already ringing.

I picked it up. "Hello," I said, still a little breathless from the jog.

"Good morning, Ms. McClanahan. Is this a good time?" The smooth, modulated voice sounded familiar, but I couldn't place it at first, and when I did my first thought was how nice of him; most doctors don't call personally.

"I have the results of the biopsy," he said.

I looked around the room, my gaze darting from one object to another, resting on the wind chime my sister-in-law had given us years before.

"I'm afraid I have some not-so-good news."

Actually, it's more than a wind chime. It's a musical instrument. Perfectly calibrated, perfectly tuned. Nine double strands of chimes. The slightest touch can set it to singing.

"Ms. McClanahan, are you there?"

Beside the wind chime is a small, gold-faced clock and two black-and-white photographs. One shows Donald's thickly tressed mother, now a decade dead from cancer, kissing her toddler son. The other is World War II vintage, my parents in profile, *locked*—there is no other word for their passion—in a kiss. The force of the kiss seems to suggest *first*, but it might also be interpreted as *last*. That's how it is with images frozen in motion, in time. Impossible to know what came just before the flash and what came after.

"When I have fears that I may cease to be . . ."

One well-known book about cancer suggests that first you cry, but I didn't. After I hung up the phone, I walked to our apartment window and looked down at the street. The vendors were out: the Korean fruit stand couple, the African sellers of purses and sunglasses, the proprietor of the umbrella-shaded Halal stand where smoke escapes in steamy wisps. A row of yellow cabs was lined up outside the Warwick Hotel, and when a man jogged past wearing a red jersey, it occurred to me that I should open the window and shout to him—about his red jersey, maybe, or about where he thought he was going. My ears felt hot. I heard a high-pitched buzzing. A mosquito? It was mid-March and I was five floors above the ground—ground that, I now realized, was spinning. My father once told me that the best thing to do when the room starts spinning is to sit still for a moment.

The List

Denial is a highly developed survival skill that has gotten a bad rap lately, and one of the best ways to deny denial is to plunge headfirst into the experience. Start by making a list. The longer the better. More items to check off.

Locate a surgeon, check. Get precertification, check. Buy new socks—colorful ones with funny pictures on them—to keep your feet warm in the hospital. Go online to research survival rates. Contact the sponsors of the readings and workshops you must postpone. Don't forget students, who will be wondering why you're canceling all those classes. To simplify things, compose a group e-mail.

"How brave you are," one friend typed back, "to face it head-on like this."

"If I ever get cancer," a student wrote, "may I take lessons from you?"

"Of course," I typed back, feeling lighter with each keystroke.

Within a few days I regretted the group e-mail. At the time, I'd thought I was being selective, but later I realized I should have told only those I know so intimately that I could have predicted their reactions. Had I done that, I would not have been ambushed by responses that, though well-intentioned, were not helpful: the colleague who knows three or four people who have had this surgery, and they're doing perfectly fine, so not to worry, this is no big deal. The friend who suggested that I plan a memorial service for the section of the colon the surgeon will remove, since it has served me so well all these years. The student who asked if she could phone me and pray aloud to God while I was on the line.

It humbles me to confess that I seriously considered the student's offer. Her e-mail arrived on a bleak morning when I had tried several times to pray on my own. On my own folded knees, with my own folded hands, my own thin, faltering voice. "Dear God," I had begun, "dear God, dear Father, oh Jesus, oh shit I am so afraid, mother of God, brother of God, sister, is anyone there?"

Gray's Anatomy

Only the frightened pray for courage or feel the need to display it. My father, the bravest man I know, cries easily. Is anyone more sentimental than an ex-marine fighter pilot? All those wars and rumors of wars, all the decades of holding it in, holding it back. One afternoon, a few days after he'd heard the news, Dad phoned me from Indiana.

"I'm so sorry you have to go through this," he sniffed. "If there's anything we can do. Anything at all." His voice began to break.

"This isn't helpful," I teased. "Put Mother on the line."

"No, I'm okay," he said, recovering himself for a moment.

Wishing to lighten the air, I decided to tell him about my appointment with the surgeon. I didn't tell him the fears I'd confided—about how long I would be under and what I prayed they wouldn't find. I didn't tell him about all the papers I'd signed—there in the surgeon's office and later at the attorney's—giving myself over to the anesthesiologists, the surgeon, and, if things did not go as planned, to Donald, my designated attorney-in-fact, who would execute my wishes.

"So I said to the surgeon, 'You're saying I'm going to have a semi-colon?'"

Dad groaned, but I kept on. "And when he told me I might have to wear a colostomy bag, I said, 'I hope not, because it's so hard to find shoes to match.'"

Dad gasped as if I'd told an off-color joke, and maybe I had. Maybe this time I'd gone too far. He probably thought that my comments showed disrespect—to myself, to my disease, to hospitals and surgeons. My father has always shown respect for the institutions of healing. Twenty years past heart valve surgery, he still wears his scar with pride. I sense, in my father, a reverence for the memory of what he calls his hospital *stay*. I don't like calling them *stays*. The same way I don't like calling airports *terminals*. I don't want to *terminate* at an airport, and I don't want to *stay* in a hospital. We should call them *visits*.

Terrifying as my father's hospital stay was, to this day he seems reluctant to let the experience die. He even saved the socks that the hospital issued him, the kind with the non-skid patches. He wears them in the morning while he works the crossword puzzle. And once a year, he stands in front of a premed class and removes his shirt while the students take notes.

Maybe I wouldn't have been making jokes if it had been my heart that was in trouble. Hearts inspire respect. Diseases of the bowel (or the colon, intestine, gut—name it what you will) do not. I have read *Illness as Metaphor*, so I realize my logic is wrong-headed. Intellectually, I agree with Sontag that "the healthiest way of being ill is one purified of metaphoric thinking." Still, I can't shake the notion that some diseases are more dignified than others. Truth be told, I was a little embarrassed at the indignity of my situation and was determined to make something from it: a metaphor, a poem, a song, something to lift me up.

"Anything you want," Donald said. "Anything." With major surgery looming in two weeks, a wiser woman might have lobbied for a post-recovery Caribbean cruise or massage coupons or at least a new silk robe. Donald got off easy. We walked to the bookstore, where I steered him toward the reference section and, sure enough, there it was: a beautiful, affordable, leather-bound copy of *Gray's Anatomy*, with gilt-edged pages and a satin ribbon secured to its spine. Though the book is only a reproduction, I liked the way it felt in my hands. Heavy, substantial. I liked the weight of history in its pages, suggesting that perhaps the body is not a complete mystery. There are those who have studied it, taken it apart, put it back together. Some of them belonged to the Royal College of Surgeons of England; why did this cheer me so? Also comforting were the black-and-white line drawings that isolate and abstract each organ, muscle, tissue, and bone. The phenoid is a monarch butterfly preparing to lift off; the choroid, an artichoke perfectly peeled, articulated; the osseous labyrinth laid open to view is part saxophone, part shell, its tip a curled wave breaking. "Look," I said to Donald, "the glands of Blandin are bristling with ducts! And just listen to the beautiful words: *capsular, synovial, navicular, subclavian*!"

Even the lowly intestine has its music. True, the poetry of the small intestine is easier to hear, with its trio of *duodenum, jejunum, ileum,* but the large intestine claims a few notes of its own: *iliac fossa, vermiform.* The caecum, I read, means "blind pouch," which translates to *cul-de-sac.*

But the real poetry of the colon lies in its movement. "The large intestine, in its course, describes an arch," is only the beginning of the story. This remarkable organ not only commences; it ascends, it bends, it flexes, it traverses, it convolutes and bends again before it descends. My tumor resided in one of these bends, the transverse arch, more specifically the splenic flexure, so named because of its proximity to the spleen. "Lucy," I imagined Ricky Ricardo saying. "You got some *'spleenin'* to do."

Maybe, I thought, I should have tried that one out on the surgeon.

GI

When I was young and my father was stationed stateside, from time to time he would announce that he was going in for "a lower GI" or, sometimes, "an upper GI." I knew that GI stands for Government Issue, which is another name for soldier, but I didn't know what an upper or lower one was, and I never asked. Not until the nurse practitioner called with instructions for my pre-op testing and directions to the "GI ward" did it dawn on me: Gastro Intestinal. I was a GI, too.

We all have ways of preparing for battle. Some drink, some cry, some sleep, some put on—in the words of whoever wrote the book of Ephesians—"the whole armor of God." My armor has always been words. Fourteen years ago, during the darkest months of separation from Donald, I frightened a therapist by grabbing up every book on her list and reading them all through, to the last bitter syllable. She kept warning me not to overdo it. "Most people read a chapter or less, that's all they can take in the midst of it," she said. Obviously she didn't know with whom she was dealing. "More books," I growled, like the Neanderthal recruit I had become.

Within days of receiving the cancer diagnosis, I started assembling my armor: books, journals, online articles. Buddhist texts on suffering. The brave, tender poems of Jane Kenyon facing cancer straight on, and losing. Even a new book by a surgeon confessing everything that can, and does, go wrong on the operating table. I placed a toy action figure on my desk, the kind that can morph into different shapes. I can do this, I thought. Bring it on.

The Creation of Adam

In a hallway off the Imaging Center, where I had come for pre-op testing, I stood beside a tall woman, both of us clutching the tops of our gowns and staring up at the huge mural. I have seen dozens of versions of Michelangelo's fresco—on stationery, aprons, even on computer mouse pads—but never one like this. This is a radiologist's version, Adam's X-rayed body open to our view: winglike clavicle, xylophone ribs, the outline of lung and heart.

The woman beside me was silent, her head cocked sideways as if expecting some message from the ceiling. I turned to her and smiled awkwardly, careful not to let my gaze wander downward. Beneath the thin gown, she was naked, as was I, but who wants to be reminded of that?

The door to the X-ray room opened, and the technician's head swiveled around the corner as if mounted on a periscope. "Next," he called, and though I was first in line, I motioned to the woman to go ahead. I wanted to spend a few more minutes with Adam.

The mural is actually two murals, the famous image split down the middle so that God and man are separated by even more distance than usual. God takes up most of the right-hand side, fully gowned and surrounded by a staff of plump, pink angels. Only his hand reaches into Adam's territory—or perhaps it is Adam who is reaching—their fingers not quite touching.

Or maybe, I imagined as I stood in the hallway, maybe they have already touched and are just now breaking away from each other. The air between them felt alive: a spark, an electrical charge, the Frankenstein juice that seemed about to jump-start Adam. Is this God energy? I wondered. Divine love that is lighting up Adam's chest, his shoulders, his heart? Then why not give us a glimpse into *God's* insides? His hidden motives, the whys and wherefores, the God heart pumping?

Every Second of Every Minute

Leaving the Imaging Center, my back to the East River, I was thinking about my mother, who, that very afternoon, was packing for her flight from Indiana to New York. At first, I had resisted offers of help from friends and family members. "When Donald goes back to work," they'd warned, "you'll need someone there." When they'd finally convinced me that this would be no picnic, that the hospital stay would be nothing compared to afterwards—"You'll be weak as a kitten," one friend said—I'd relented.

So now my seventy-eight-year-old mother—the daughter of farmers, grandmother of fifteen, and president of the local quilting club, whose members, seated around the frame at last week's meeting, had warned her of the city's dangers, advising her to pin her Social Security card and cash inside her brassiere—was suiting up for battle.

I passed the subway entrance on Sixty-Eighth Street, opting to walk the two miles to our apartment. I'd chosen the residential route, row after row of townhouses where miniature gardens are locked behind wrought iron. In one garden, aucuba bushes were pushing up against the gate, their raucous green and yellow streaks sending my mind back to the old house in North Carolina where we'd lived when we were first married, the massive bushes no amount of neglect could kill—they just kept growing, pushing up against the house—and then there in the next garden arrived another life, this one hidden in Japanese pieris, those same delicate clusters that had softened the entry to the first home we'd mortgaged our future to buy, and in their blooms were all the years we'd spent there—planting, cooking, sleeping, loving—and what if, I was thinking, what if? Then I was moving faster, my heels clicking on the sidewalk as I hurried across the avenues—First, Second, Third, Lexington, Park, Madison, Fifth—feeling dizzier with each step.

Then, finally, there was Central Park, where I could sit a minute.

Most of the benches that line the South Pond bear commemorative plaques. There is one from Barbara to Marty in celebration of their wedding anniversary, another from a family reminding us that even in the aftermath of 9/11, we can still find refuge among these trees and flowers. Many of the inscriptions are as simple and clear-cut as gravestones, marking the parameters of a life: "For our beloved brother, son and friend, 1958–1996." A few are enigmatic. "For Noodling," reads one. "Entirely of possibility," another.

My favorite bench, the one on which I had once again landed, proclaims "Every second of every minute. August 7, 1997–." I like that there is no closing date, that the inscription celebrates only a beginning. A baby was born on that date, perhaps, or a love affair started, a marriage began. Or maybe that was the day someone's life took a turn. A divorce decree was final, a son buried a father, the lab tests came back—all the things we call endings that could also be seen as beginnings. The way liberated prisoners claim a new birthday. The way, on some board games, you can place your marker on any space. Choose: start here.

Dream after Reading Gray's Anatomy

Inside the gold-rimmed hospital, we wear the shape of our diseases. In the cardiac ward, the valentine woman. In the circulatory ward, the highway map man. And here in the GI ward, we are navy, lima, kidney, all manner of beans coiled into ourselves. Cul-de-sacs. Pink kangaroo nurses hop from bed to bed, adjusting their pouches.

The Waiting Room

Patients-in-waiting are easy to spot. We are the ones wearing non-skid socks and large cotton robes over loose pajamas, so as to cover all bases. Except for our bare, nervous hands, patients-in-waiting hold nothing in our laps, our belongings having been stashed in official brown paper bags marked with the hospital's name.

I had been ordered to report mid-morning and I had been waiting nearly two hours, Donald to the left of me, Mother to the right, a television mounted high on the wall in front of us. A noose was looped around the neck of a huge Saddam Hussein statue, and a tiny marine was climbing onto its face and draping it in an American flag.

I knew I should have been more interested—this was, after all, history in the making, a regime tumbling—but my gaze kept wandering to the window, where, a dozen stories below, a barge was making its slow, determined way along the East River. Does the barge move on its own power, I wondered, or do the currents help it along? As I watched, it passed under the Queensboro Bridge, then beneath that little cable-car-in-the-sky that floats its passengers to and from Roosevelt Island. When Donald and I were planning our move to New York, we'd briefly considered living there but decided no. "It feels like a hospital," Donald said. "Because it was," I said. Decades ago, the whole island had been comprised of institutions, including the New York City Lunatic Asylum, where Mae West was briefly incarcerated after appearing in what was then judged to be a lewd play. As the story goes, she convinced the powers-that-be to allow her to wear her silk underwear beneath the prison garb.

I walked to the window and looked across the river: Roosevelt Island. Named for a president who never let his legs show in published photos. Only in candid shots with family and friends did he allow the camera its full range. What was he afraid of? I wondered. That he would lose his power if the public got a good look at the whole man, folded into a wheelchair or leaning on the arms of those he loved? As I padded across the room, I felt the grab of the sock treads against the floor. I'd tried to sneak out of the changing room wearing the bright pink flamingo socks I'd bought the week before, but the attendant had sent me back for the official hospital footwear.

Mother smiled up at me, and I took my seat between her and Donald, crossing my arms on the stiff fabric. In a pathetic attempt at style, I had rolled up the huge sleeves and the long pant legs and sashed the robe twice. I should have insisted on silk underwear—Mae West had the right idea—embroidered with my name, perhaps. Some small comfort, something of myself to keep on "my person," as the attendant called what was left of me after I'd stepped out of the changing room. In an ideal world, a patient would be allowed to bring along all the accoutrements that make up her person. A gardener could pack a shovel and her best petunia bed; a grandfather, photographs of the grandchildren; a writer, all the books she has read and the ones she has written. The body of her work. Her corpus.

Instead, they strip you bare, and last to go are the rings that link you to the one you love. During my father's hospitalization, my mother wore his wedding ring on a chain around her neck. Donald and I had never worn wedding bands, but he'd surprised me with two diamonds, one on our fifteenth anniversary and one on our twenty-fifth. Before we'd left the apartment for the hospital that morning, I'd planted both rings in an envelope in his dresser, tucked inside a letter marked "Special Bequests" that detailed all the little things that hadn't made it into the official documents we'd signed the week before. By the time we'd left the lawyer's office, my hands were trembling, my mouth dry. Marriage vows are nothing compared to death vows, signing yourself over. Terror more binding than any "I do," this power to connect, disconnect.

Donald nudged me, and I looked up at the television. The statue was tipping forward, yanked from its moorings by tiny men with ropes—a scene out of *Gulliver's Travels*. "End of an era," the reporter announced.

And the huge body toppled.

The Pain Guys

Three young men, joined at the clipboard, appeared at the foot of my stretcher in the area where patients are held before surgery. "We're the pain team," one of them announced. In all my planning, my careful research, I must have missed something. Were they telling me this was going to hurt?

They could have been movie stars or fashion models, but no, of course they wanted to be doctors. Feeling suddenly old, I tilted my chin and flashed them my best smile. "The nurse has already been here," I said, lifting both hands to show where she had "introduced" IV lines. One was hooked to a drip bag; the other, capped and taped, had been readied for the anesthesia.

One of the pain guys checked the clipboard, the second checked my IV sites, and the third started explaining the epidural they were about to administer. Epidural? I thought. Isn't that for women in labor? My sisters had epidurals.

The third pain guy asked me to sit up, then positioned me so that my legs were hanging off the side of the bed. "Lean forward," he commanded. "That's good." He started tapping on my vertebra as if looking for a tender spot. He asked the second pain guy for his opinion. This did not inspire confidence. Maybe I had been wrong to choose a teaching hospital.

"Can't you just knock me out?" I said. "A hammer will be fine."

He pushed my head down gently. "Just lean over a little more. That's great," he said. "That's good. Just hold that position. You'll feel some pressure now."

I told them that there was no need for this, that I didn't plan on using the epidural.

"Right," the third pain guy smirked.

"I don't do well with drugs," I said. "Never have. They make me stupid. And nauseous. I won't be using this."

"Time will tell," the first guy answered, moving around the stretcher and standing in front of me. I figured he wanted to check my mouth, to measure it for the endotracheal—the tube that would breathe for me while my chest muscles were paralyzed and my mind was who-knows-where for three hours, four, five. And what if the anesthesia is more than a dream? I thought. What if I don't wake up?

I opened my mouth as wide as I could. He just stared at me. "We're the *pain* team," he said. "For afterwards."

Later, after they had gone and the nurse had come yet again to check my blood pressure and IV, she showed me the magic button that I could push when the pain got too much.

"Now?" I smiled, pretending to scramble for the button.

She narrowed her eyes. Most nurses are great kidders, but this one was an exception.

The afternoon dragged on. Mother and Donald took turns sitting on the little plastic stool. Gurneys were wheeled in and out. The minute hand on the big school clock stuttered and jumped. The nurse kept saying, "Just a little while longer," and, "They're readying the O.R. right now."

Finally, at nearly five o'clock, an orderly appeared.

"Cocktail hour?" I said.

The orderly was a moon-faced woman with round eyes and plump hands. She placed a blue paper cap over my hair, checked my ID bracelet, and leaned over to unlock the wheels. Mother reached over and touched my forehead, Donald kissed me on the cheek, and I lay back, blinking against the brightness of the ceiling lights. Now we were moving, the IV pole rolling beside us, really moving, out of the holding room, through the swinging double doors into a corridor, another, and now we were wheeling down a long hallway, window after window flashing past. I turned my head to the right and saw a slice of silver water, another slice, another. "Slow down," I said. "I want to see the river."

The orderly not only slowed, she stopped.

"Take a good look, honey," she said softly.

I was not prepared for such kindness, or for the dazzling water, hundreds of white lights winking back at us. What a stunning sight, and what if, what if, I thought, but it was too late for that now; we were moving again, down the long hallway, where a brawny nurse was waiting beside a short, dark man outside the O.R. doors. He asked me a few questions, pointed to a clipboard, and told me to sign here, and here.

"Wait," I said. I'd seen this on a documentary once, and it made sense. "Tell me my name. Tell me what operation I'm having."

He answered correctly on both counts. I asked him the name of my surgeon, just to be sure. Again he answered correctly.

"Okay," I said, and signed on the dotted lines.

"Thou preparest a table before me . . ."

I remember how big and white the room was, how bright the overhead lights shining on all that metal, and how small the table looked. The table spread for me, on which I would be spread. The anesthesiologist, another young man—why are they all so young? I thought—leaned over and asked me how much I weighed. Then he asked me to open my mouth so he could measure for the endotracheal. He sighed, and I wondered if he was thinking how small my throat was, how hard it would be to insert the tube; thank God I'd be asleep when he did that. I wanted to pray, but nothing original would come. "The Lord is my shepherd," I began silently. Green coats were gathering in my peripheral vision. I heard feet shuffling, hushed voices.

"You'll feel a cold sensation," the anesthesiologist said. What a terrible job to have, I thought. What could be worse than putting someone under? Surely goodness and mercy shall follow me, I continued, imagining three little sheep behind the shepherd—Shirley in the lead, Goodness and Mercy padding, on cottony feet, closely behind.

"May I count?" I asked. When I was small the dentist always told me to count backward starting with ten. But that was a long time ago.

"One hundred," I began. "Ninety-nine. Ninety-eight. Ninety-seven."

Roommates

Twin bed, single bed, the terms are used interchangeably, but between them lies a vast difference. Twin is what you sleep in when you are young. Across the room in the other twin bed is your sister, so close that you can reach out and touch her if you need to, and some nightmare nights you do. Twin suggests that half of you exists in another. You are a matched set, your separateness chosen rather than required.

There are no twin beds in hospitals. Each one, narrow and white and tagged with a name, is a single.

Even if you are lucky enough to have a husband and a mother standing beside you when you wake in the recovery room.

Even if you are lucky enough, as I was that first night, to be wheeled from recovery into a semi-private room where a wise woman lay in the other single bed. A woman whose name would escape me for days, another side effect of the anesthesia. I, who have always prided myself on my memory—what a strange phrase, *to pride oneself*, as if there were two selves, one who does the boasting and the other who accepts the compliment—found that I would begin a thought that I could not finish until much later. Sharon, her name was, or something like that. A pretty name, easy on the ears. A name spoken, from behind the curtain that separated us, in a voice that came as close to soothing as any voice could have, considering my pounding head, the convulsive trembling and post-anesthesia nausea, the wretched dry heaves.

"I'm sorry," I managed, after another violent bout of gagging and heaving.

"It's okay," the voice behind the curtain answered. "You'll be better tomorrow. You'll turn a corner."

Sharon's corner had already been turned; the doctor would sign the papers the next day so that she could go home. In the meantime, there was this night to get through. Anyone who thinks you can rest in a hospital has never spent a night in one. If you manage, through the mercy of pills or exhaustion, to doze off for a moment, you will be roused by a blood-taker, an IV-checker, a catheter-emptier, or a Voice crying out. I capitalize *Voice* because the Voice seemed larger and more terrible than any body to which it could have been attached. The man's cries, issuing from somewhere down the hall, came in waves, every two or three hours, followed by a woman's voice—his wife's, I imagined—cooing and crooning to no effect. Nothing, it seemed, could ease his cries. I have never heard such agony and hope never to again.

"Bless him," Sharon whispered from behind the curtain. I did not yet know the seriousness of her prognosis, what she was facing. Had I known, I like to think I would have tried to comfort her, though, in the state I was in, I cannot be sure. If there is a scale of suffering—and I am certain there is—it is impossible to gauge your place on that scale when you are in the midst of suffering, however minor your suffering might appear in retrospect. All that long night and the next day, I could not lift my head, but I could turn it on the pillow and watch Sharon move past my bed and to the bathroom. Amazing, I thought, to lift your body from the bed, to move on your own power, without IV lines and catheter. To sit on the toilet. To flush. How amazing. I heard the spray of the shower through the walls, and when the bathroom door opened, a fresh, clean smell emerged and clung to her as she moved toward the window or out into the hallway, where she began yet another slow circle around the nurses' station.

By the end of the second day, I could smell the sourness of my sweat and sickness, my rancid breath. Every few hours, the nurses' aide would appear at the door, announcing that I needed a wash, that this was her job, and that I should let her do it. She was a light-skinned black woman with short red hair and an attitude so outwardly crusty that I knew she was hiding something soft inside. I wanted to please her, I wanted a bath, but I could not lift my head without the room spinning and the bile backing up in my throat. She would stare down at me, shake her head, and then turn and walk out of the room, saying to the air, "That one won't let me do nothing for her. Nothing at all."

Sharon had brought her own robe from home, and terry cloth slippers that shuffled and scuffed as she moved herself along. On her own power, I kept thinking. Someone moving on her own power. I wondered why no one was there with her. Would she be going home alone? Her stomach was huge, the sash of the robe tied high between breasts and belly, the way you tie a maternity dress. But she was older than I was, too old to be pregnant.

It wasn't until later that evening, when the doctor came to sign her out, that I learned the nature and extent of her disease. I wasn't trying to listen, but semi-private means just that. As close as you are in your single beds, no secrets can be kept. So I learned that her cancer was far advanced, that she had been in the hospital more times than she could count, and that she would be back again in a few weeks. "Not that it will do a lot of good in the long run, you understand that, don't you, Renée?" the doctor was saying.

Renée. Yes, that was her name; it was finally coming back to me. I now wish I had learned her last name so that I could send her a letter of thanks. If I could trace her. If she is still alive. There is a Japanese artist at the edge of the park who can write your name on a grain of rice. That is what he claims. I have never stopped at his booth, but I believe he can do exactly that. Maybe that is why I have never stopped.

Corpus

By the end of the third day, I could sit up on the bed, my legs wrapped in compression boots, my head held over a plastic tub while I brushed my teeth. Has anything ever felt so good? I could sip water through a straw and suck on ice chips, which soothed my throat, still raw from the intubation. The anti-nausea drip had kicked in, so I had even slept a few hours. This isn't so bad, I thought. This is manageable.

That was before the anesthesia wore off and the pain from the incision began.

That was before I was told the pathology report wasn't in yet.

That was before the second roommate was wheeled in, a thin woman with prominent cheekbones and a voice like a saw. All day, all night, it scraped and rasped and scraped some more. Even my mother and Donald, both eternally patient, began to chafe against the sound.

The next morning, the rounds began.

"The incision looks good," the surgeon announced, "but you don't. I heard you had some trouble with the anesthesia."

The internist stopped by. "Why aren't you up? You need to start moving. Have you passed gas yet?" I knew that this was my ticket out. If I did not pass Gas, I could not collect two hundred dollars. I could not be released. And God knows I wanted to be released.

The three pain guys showed up. "How often are you pushing the pain button?"

"It makes me sick, I told you that."

They shook their handsome heads, made notes on their

clipboards. "You know if you don't use the button, you will experience—"

"Pain," I snapped. "I know."

The resident team appeared at the door, a multicolored clump of men and women. One of them turned and spoke to the others. "Caucasian woman, aged fifty-two, presenting with . . ." Presenting with? Where were my tap shoes, my top hat and cane? And now, folks, from behind the curtain, here she is. Now presenting . . .

A body that has not been bathed in three days. A helmet of oily, matted hair. Feet that must belong to Petunia Pig. Tubes for arms, a catheter tail. Newly rearranged bowels that have not passed gas. A swollen belly stitched together, hanging by a thread. Jesus, what a body of work. Body of work, my corpus.

Your Name on a Grain of Rice

That evening, after Donald and Mother left for home (which in my pride and stubbornness I insisted they do), the roommate's sawing began in earnest and did not let up. She talked to the air, to herself, to her missing daughter, to the faces at the window, the faces she claimed were peering in at her. Imagining what Renée would have done, I spoke. "It's okay, it's okay. There's no one at the window." Behind the curtain, the woman gasped; I must have frightened her. Then, from down the hall, the Voice cried out. Agony no one could ease. No matter how hard you try, you cannot get inside someone else's pain.

And no one can get inside yours. Lying there, exhausted and terrified—though the surgeon reported that the site had looked clean to him, the pathology report was still not back, and I was starting to imagine the worst—I tried every mind trick I knew, every technique I had been taught in hospice volunteer training all those years before. Techniques I had enthusiastically passed on to the patients as if I knew what they were feeling. I tried visualizing a beautiful place: a waterfall, the meadow behind my grandparents' farm, the view of Central Park's South Pond from my favorite bench. I tried going back in time, but moments were slippery and would not hold. I tried reciting the dozens of poems I knew by heart. Or thought I knew. Emerson, Roethke, Hopkins, Yeats, where had they gone? I could not even call forth my own poems. Words and phrases would emerge in my mind's periphery, then float past before I could grab their sense. Nothing makes sense, when you stop to think about it. Why do we say, of someone who has killed herself, "She was a suicide," but not, of someone who has had cancer, "She was a cancer"? Why do we pray for negative pathology reports and fear positive ones? "On the verge," we write, but how can we tell when we are on it? And a "sleepless night"? The night is not sleepless. Just us, wrapped too tightly in it. Shirley, Goodness, and Mercy shall follow me, but who are they anyway, I wondered, and why were they following me, little dream sheep nipping at my heels?

Then, as I lay on the sweaty hospital sheets, here came the parade of single words—each one lonely, discrete—appearing on the screen in my mind's eye, then breaking apart, the connective tissue tearing loose until only the skeleton of the word was revealed, as if lit from behind:

about a bout (the battle we fight)

knowledge ledge of know (over which we tumble).

Suddenly I could see the moth hidden inside *mother*. Virginia Woolf's moth, dazed and exhausted, beating its wings against the window.

Down the hall, a sound wave was breaking, and the Voice was crying out. Suffering no one could ease. Not the nurses who hurried past my door, or the doctors who answered the summons, or the wife whose voice echoed his cries, singing back in a language composed entirely of vowels. Their voices broke, rose and fell, crashed against the rock of silence, and then broke again in an opera of shared pain.

Body of Work

God, we are told, is a god of mercy and compassion. But this belief lets no one off the hook. Not God, not us. Scratch its surface, and you expose its smaller, harder core: that the unmerciful exists in the first place. If suffering did not exist, God would not be forced to be merciful and compassionate. He could use his energies in other ways. He would not have to be on call, day and night, minute by minute.

For, finally, that is the promise. Not that God will relieve the suffering, but that we will not have to do this alone. We will have company. Not Michelangelo's plump, pink angels, perhaps, but company all the same. For me, the night nurses whose backlit forms appeared in the doorway. The aides who removed the catheter and collected toilet samples and plumped the pillow and changed the sheets. The blood technicians who tried their best, who poked and missed and poked again: "Sorry, I didn't mean to hurt you." The food workers with foreign accents who brought trays with Jell-O and juice, Jell-O and juice, Jell-O and applesauce and juice. The two teenage volunteers, beautiful Asian girls, who rolled the cart of library books to the foot of my bed and were so intent on making me smile that, though words had still not returned to me, I chose three books anyway, solely for the bright colors on their covers. A husband who brought news from home, and cards and flowers, who watched for the IV's final drip and pressed the call button. An aging mother on whose arm I leaned as I hobbled past the nurses' station, holding my incision, letting out little kitten whimpers I hoped no one could hear, because I had nothing to whimper about, I who would be released in a day or two because I was now a virtual whoopee cushion, my body of work reduced to a series of punctuation marks, exclamation point after exclamation point, each more welcome than the next. I, who had been bathed and freshly powdered, who could hobble on my own power, dragging my IV pole past the nurses' station, past the room of the Voice that was now too quiet, down the corridor to the window where the East River flowed and thousands of lights from thousands of windows blinked back at me.

Back

Each day I grew a little stronger. That first day home, Palm Sunday, I staggered into the apartment and fell into the sheets Donald had turned back for me. Hours later, when I woke, a phone was ringing somewhere in the distance, and Mother's voice was answering, but not in words. It was as if I were underwater, just below the surface: all was tone, music, lilt and fall. I tried to lift my head, but my friend had been right; I *was* weak as a kitten. Later I woke shivering, and someone came in to arrange the down comforter over me. When I woke again I was sweating, but I could not move the comforter—it was too heavy—so I mewed (*the three little kittens have lost their mittens*) for my mother, and she came to lift first the comforter, then me.

Over the next few days, Mother began leaving the door to the bedroom open, as if inviting me back into the world. But the view from my bed was almost too much to take in. The photographs of my nephews and nieces. The lamp with the pink shade lighting the watercolor painted by my aunt, who, in her ninety years on this earth, had survived betrayal, divorce, subsequent happiness, widowhood, and innumerable surgeries and recoveries. The bookcase, its two rows devoted to the twenty—count them, twenty!—gilt-embossed dictionaries. How could one alphabet take up so much space?

And there, in the leather reading chair, was a section of my mother. I couldn't see all of her from the bed, but I trusted that she was complete. Each time the phone rang, I watched her hand pick up the receiver and press it to her ear. I was happy that the phone was ringing, that someone out there somewhere wished me well, but I was too exhausted to even imagine talking. What words would I use?

To keep my mind occupied, and in an attempt to jump-start my brain, I had gathered books around me. The novels and biographies served mostly as props, but the poems, with their open meadows of white space, were almost navigable. I began with haiku by Issa and Masahide, then slowly worked my way, line by line, toward my favorite longer poems: "I learn by going where I have to go" (Roethke). "When I have fears that I may cease to be" (Keats). And some lines by my late friend, William Matthews:

> Anyone proud of his brain should try to drag
> his body with him before bragging.

The lines are from "Recovery Room," a poem that turns, as many of Bill's poems turn, on a phrase. In this case, its final line:

Welcome back, somebody said. Back? Back?

Because of course the speaker of Bill's poem knew—as Bill knew, as anyone who has ever gone through the valley of the shadow knows—that there is no *back*. When you return, if you return, everything is changed. The light, the music. It is too bright, perhaps, or too noisy. Too something. You feel exposed, unprotected, so what else to do but re-cover? Cover yourself over, again. You can't stay naked forever, stripped bare, all your fears revealed, your insides lit up.

I have the X-rays to prove it. And the excellent negative report from the pathologists. A year past surgery, I am writing these words with a pen that bears the name of the hospital, a souvenir from my stay. I now understand why no one calls them visits; no matter how long since my release, part of me remains there. I am beginning to understand why my father still wears those tacky little socks and still opens his shirt for the premed students. I threw my hospital socks away, but I did save the pen. And one memory that, try as I might, I can't seem to shake. It was the fourth day after surgery. Donald and Mother had just left for lunch, and, at my request, the privacy curtain had been arranged on its metal rings so that it formed an enclosure around my bed. Inside that enclosure, I lay on the sweaty, rumpled sheets, my oily hair plastered to my forehead, my eyes closed against the overhead light. I heard the squeak of metal, and there she stood: the light-skinned aide with the short red hair and the crusty manner. She was carrying a small plastic tub into which she had placed a washcloth, a hotel size bar of soap, and sample size containers of baby powder and lotion. Over one arm, she had draped a towel.

"I'm not taking no for an answer," she said.

She removed the items from the tub, arranging them neatly on the night table. Then she carried the tub to the sink and filled it with water, returning to place it on the table. She helped me out of bed and placed a stool in the space beside my bed.

"Sit," she said.

The rest was accomplished mostly in silence, an awkward dance of stretch and lift, untie, remove, soap and rinse, cream and pat and powder, and all the while my tears were falling—into the plastic tub, down my cheeks and breasts, onto the surgical tape that held my swollen belly together. She handed me a sponge and motioned for me to do the rest. There are limits even for bathers, parts of ourselves that only we can be responsible for.

When I was finished, she held up a clean, stiff gown, and I found my way into it. Then, while I sat on the stool, cradling my incision, she stripped the bed of its sheets, the pillow of its white casing. This is what they do when someone doesn't wake up, I thought.

But I had woken up. The bed looked so empty, and for an instant—very quickly, then it was gone—I felt a sting, a pinch of grief for the one who had so recently lain there. The tears started again. I had not cried like this since I was a child. She just stood there and let me do it. I started to thank her, but I knew that if I started thanking, I would never stop. As if sensing this, she held up both hands like a cop directing traffic. Then she reached for a clean sheet, flung it over the bed, and tucked in the edges, taking extra care to center the top sheet and the freshly cased pillow, which she fluffed and fluffed, looking my way.

Early Morning, Downtown 1 Train

IN THIS CAR PACKED with closed faces, this tube of light tunneling through darkness: two sleeping boys, so close I could touch them without reaching—their smooth brown faces, planed cheekbones like Peruvian steps leading from or to some beautiful ruin. Boys so alike they must be brothers. And the small, worried man they sprawl against, too young to seem so old? Father.

How far have they come? How far to go? They sleep as only loved children sleep, wholly, no need to tighten or clutch, to fold themselves in. Their heads are thrown back, mouths open—no, agape, which looks like *agape*, the highest form of love, some minister told me long ago. As if love is a cupboard of lower and higher shelves, and why bother reaching if you have hands like the hands of this young father, cracked and blistered, stamped with the pattern of shovel or pick.

For someone must do our digging, and rise in the dark to dress the children carefully, as these boys are dressed, and pack their knapsacks, and ease out of the seat without waking the open-mouthed younger one nor the older, whose head now rests fully on the emptied seat . . . but, my God, I am thinking, as the train brakes squeal and the father moves quickly to face the door, he is leaving these children, a father is leaving his children.

The train slows at Fiftieth and he presses his body against the door, lifting his arms above his head—a signal? surrender?—as the door slides open and a woman steps in, small and dark like the father, her body lost in a white uniform. She touches his sleeve, something passes between their eyes. Not sadness exactly, but ragged exhaustion, frayed edges meeting: his night her day, her night his day, *goodbye hello*.

She slides onto the seat, lifting one son's head to her lap. His mouth is still open, his body limp. She smooths his collar. Her small hands move to his lips, closing them gently, the way one closes the mouth of the recently dead. But the boy is not dead. Just sleeping, an arm thrown over his brother. His mother near.

Adopt a Bench

NOT EVERYONE CAN AFFORD to adopt a Central Park bench and personalize it with a plaque, but it costs nothing to sit on one. My favorite bench at Conservatory Water is inscribed with "Tell Me Something You Promised You Wouldn't Tell" and dedicated to a woman named Helen, who lived for nearly a century. Helen must have been very rich or very loved, perhaps both; several benches bear her name or initials, along with snippets of poems, such as "Hushing my deepest grief of all / And filled with tears that cannot fall," a bastardization of Tennyson's famous lines for his dead friend. I think of tears that cannot fall, how much it hurts to hold them back, to dam up all that grief. A few weeks after the towers fell, I dreamed that thousands of New Yorkers were kneeling beside the Hudson River, our fingers plugging up holes in a dike that was about to break.

Since all of Helen's benches are taken this morning, and since I prefer to sit undisturbed, with my notebook and pen, I have no choice but to take up residence on the one empty bench left, near the concession stand. "Best Mom," the inscription reads. My husband waves from across the pond; his miniature sailboat, a modest boat by Central Park standards, is holding its own. Donald bought it secondhand not long after we moved to the city, and he added a yellow ducky decal to get the kids' attention so they'll grab their fathers' hands and tug them away from the Sunday *Times*. Though we're decades past the possibility of having children of our own, Donald remains a Pied Piper. Kids will follow him anywhere.

I wave back to him and settle onto the bench. Here in Conservatory Water (I once mistyped it as "Conversatory Water," which is absolutely what I'm trying to avoid, conversing) all the benches face the pond. Unlike on the subway, where you're forced to look either down into your lap or into the eyes of the commuter across from you, here your eyes can rest on the remote-controlled sailboats tacking into the late June wind, or on the birders with their binoculars and tripod telescopes trained high on spots in the buildings and trees. I take my notebook from my bag. It's been months since a poem seized me, but early this morning I'd felt a slight stirring, a breeze ruffling the edges of sleep, a dream of Caribou Man. Not that the legendary Inuit would pay me a personal visit, cynic that I am and skeptic of all things ghostly. Still, ever since my trip to the Museum of the American Indian last week, Caribou Man has been loitering in the shadows of my thoughts.

I hear the squeak of wheels and sense a presence in my periphery, a large-bodied someone approaching my bench. Usually it's best not to acknowledge a stranger; you might get a talker. Plus, this stranger has a peculiar odor—not a stench exactly, but a musty, used-up smell. The bench vibrates as the person sits down. I hear some clicking, a beep or two, and then a distant, automated female voice: "What listing?"

"D'Agostino. On Seventy-Sixth and Lexington," answers the deep, gruff voice beside me.

"We're sorry, but we show no listing—"

"I will keep interrupting until I get a real person," the gruff voice says.

"We're sorry, but we show no listing—"

"I will keep interrupting until I get a real person." He does not raise his voice or seem the least bit flustered, just patiently insistent. This could go on all morning.

I sense that he is looking at me. "You can't even get a number from directory service," he says. So far I've glimpsed only bare ankles and badly scuffed leather loafers, probably Italian, the kind Donald sometimes tries on in expensive stores and then denies himself. "You pay for the service and you can't get a number."

I should turn toward him, to see what I've gotten myself into, and also to prove that I am a real person. Instead, I return to my notebook and Caribou Man. Depending on which legend you buy into, a Naskapi tribesman was visited in a dream by a caribou doe that beckoned to him, and because dreams trump waking life in Naskapi culture, the tribesman followed her. But unlike the speaker of Walt Whitman's poem, who only imagined "I could turn and live with animals," the tribesman actually did it. He joined the herd, covering himself in caribou hides, grazing on moss alongside his adopted brothers, and sleeping close to them at night. One legend says he left because his wife claimed he was a rotten husband; in another version, his human wife and son track him across the snow, losing his trail when his footprints morph into hoofprints. Believers in the myth claim Caribou Man is still wandering.

The man on the bench won't give up. He dials and speaks, dials and speaks. I have to admire his persistence. I look up from my notebook. "It *is* frustrating," I say, "to get a machine." That's when I see his cut-off—or, more precisely, rip-off—khakis, frayed at the bottoms. He wears a white dress shirt buttoned all the way up, with a tie clip of Kermit the Frog attached to the collar. A once-elegant dinner jacket completes the ensemble—no, not quite completes, I see now, as my eyes take in a speckled gray pigeon perched on the man's shoulder.

"I might have the spelling wrong," he says. He asks me how to spell D'Agostino. I know the grocery chain, but I've never shopped there. We tease it out for a while: is the *d* followed by an *a* or an *o*? And where does the apostrophe go? Is that Italian mark even called an apostrophe?

The man stands and walks behind the bench. The pigeon does not budge. Is it Velcroed to his shoulder? Wheels squeak, and a shopping cart emerges, overflowing with clothes, shoes, a toaster, a vintage adding machine. I look away so he won't catch me staring. He rummages in the cart.

"I should have saved my last receipt," he says. "I don't beg, you understand. But I do get hungry. I have to eat. A lot. Every day." His hand is still in the cart, foraging. "They put the phone number on the receipt, you know."

"You could write the number down and carry it with you," I say. "For the next time."

"That's a great idea," he says. His hands disappear into the cart again, and he pulls out a notebook almost identical to mine. He and the Velcroed pigeon return to the bench, where the man opens the notebook and flips through a few pages until he comes to a list—handwritten, with clear, beautiful penmanship, the kind you hardly ever see anymore. It occurs to me that this strange, pungent-smelling man has a history. He was a schoolboy once. Some teacher or mother or father stood beside him, perhaps guiding his hand to show him how to form the letters—*his* letters:

that's the way teachers used to say it. "Rebecca needs help in forming her letters," my first grade teacher wrote in a report card note to my mother, as if the letters belonged only to me, as if only I could bring them to life.

Looking close, I can make out a few names beside phone numbers on the man's list: "Chase Manhattan," "Greyhound," "Amtrak (Julie)." I know Amtrak Julie. I call her now and then to check on trains. The real Julie was on *Jeopardy!* once, and it felt strange to see a body attached to the familiar voice. Maybe my benchmate doesn't know Amtrak Julie is a recording. Maybe he calls her just to hear her voice, so warm and perky, reassuring and polite. She'd probably let you talk until you wore yourself out.

∽∽

"I would have done anything to save you," reads one of four benches on the north side of the pond. The benches are the standard Adopt-A-Bench style. Price: $7,500. I know because I did the research a few years ago, right before my cancer surgery. I'd been advised to update my will, to give Donald power of attorney in case something "unexpected" occurred while I was on the table. At the lawyer's office I seriously contemplated adding a bench adoption to my will. When you consider that the cost covers maintenance for as long as the park survives (a strange thought, isn't it, that a park could ever die?) $7,500 isn't an exorbitant price.

I got as far as the adoption form, hesitating only at the inscription line. The problem is, whatever inscription you choose lasts forever, like a tattoo, only more permanent; a tattoo can be removed. Finally I decided against the bench.

I don't even want to decide what to carve on my headstone. Leave that to my survivors.

∞

The wind has picked up, and Donald's boat is struggling, its sail listing deeply. Across the pond, kids are climbing on the Hans Christian Andersen statue. The bronze storyteller holds a giant copy of *The Ugly Duckling* while the duckling himself gazes up in admiration. Nearby, the birders are aiming their telescopes toward the twelfth-floor balcony of 927 Fifth Avenue in hopes of catching a glimpse of the red-tailed hawk known as Pale Male—in the act of conjugal passion, perhaps, or a morning meal of fresh rat. I've always thought it strange that the hawk could find so many rats in such a fancy neighborhood, but I guess there are plenty of rats to go around. Pigeons, too.

I've spotted Pale Male only once, swooping across the model boat pond, his unusually light-colored feathers a Sunday miracle cheered on by onlookers. I've seen screech owls, too, and once a Cooper's hawk, but the red-tailed is the king.

"Enjoy the fake nature," a Birkenstocked, backpacking woman once shouted at me as I was entering the park and she was exiting. Had she been expecting the Grand Tetons or something? I wanted to shout back, The rocks aren't fake. Have you sat on one? They're real glacial outcroppings, some of them. Sure, they were brought here, but they're still ancient, as ancient as they'd be anywhere else. The raccoons are real too, and the opossums and cottontails and squirrels. And if that coyote strolls through again, don't pet him, okay? Because he's real too. What did she expect? Olmstead and Vaux did the best they could to create a wild place in the center of civilization—or a civilization in the midst of all the wildness, which is how Central Park has always felt to me.

∞

My seatmate has been quiet for too long. Did he give up on directory assistance? Have I hurt his feelings by not engaging? The pigeon is still there, head bobbing, wings tucked in. It doesn't coo, but now and then a burbling sound erupts from its throat, like a soft engine starting up in the distance. The man nods, as if he understands what the pigeon is saying.

"How long have you had the pigeon?" I ask.

"Seven nights," he says, and he's off and running, words tumbling ahead of him while he chases after. He was playing guitar outside the Met—he's a musician—and the rain started, and she swooped down and landed on his shoulder and just stayed. "Like Baby," he says, pointing behind the bench.

I turn to see a strange-looking dog—a Welsh corgi? No, my brother has a corgi, but this dog looks more like a . . .

"Half German Shepherd, half dachshund," the man says, as if to answer my furrowed brow. "I got her in California. People laugh me out of the park when I say that, the thought that those two breeds could ever get together . . ."

I try to picture the doggy gymnastics but can get only so far. I suppose there are even stranger couplings. Avid birders in the park swear they once saw a tufted titmouse sitting on the rump of a raccoon, plucking fur to use in its nest. The raccoon just sat there and let the bird do it.

Studying the dog closer, I don't doubt the man's story:

the large face, the big ears, the squat legs, the long torso. I ask him how old Baby is.

"Seven months yesterday," he tells me. "Born on Thanksgiving Day." He celebrates every month, does something special for her, like dog treats from D'Agostino. "D'Agostino is the best. They deliver. Costs ten more dollars, but it's worth it. They're good about bringing it right to my cart."

"That's great," I say, thinking, How in the world can he afford it? He must sleep in the park, maybe in the isolated woods near the old fort.

"I celebrate her birthday every month, because who knows how long she will last. Maybe it's for me, the celebration. Just something small. To mark the occasion."

A bench. He needs to adopt a bench for Baby so that her name can live on, like the names of the dogs on so many park benches: Biscuit, Truffle, Daisy, Earl the Pearl. I close my notebook, having given up on Caribou Man for today. Lots of people are out, real live people, and the kids are lining up at the telescope to catch a glimpse of Pale Male. A little girl has escaped from her mother's lap and is climbing onto the Ugly Duckling, hugging his neck so tightly she'd strangle him if he were real.

Of course the little girl knows he isn't real. But she might not know that the Ugly Duckling wasn't a duckling at all. He was a cygnet whose egg had accidentally found its way into a mother duck's nest. I used to wonder why the sculptor commemorated the opening of the book rather than the end. Wouldn't most viewers prefer a beautiful swan to a homely cygnet? Then it came to me: the point of Andersen's story isn't some Disneyesque miracle—*voila*, you're a swan, now you can soar with the others above your troubled life!—but rather the history of the bird's longing, his journey of loneliness, the long, dark winter when he wandered, lost between worlds, letting out a cry so high that it terrified him with its strangeness, until his pulsing heart could take no more, and he cried out, "Kill me!" to the beautiful swans swooping toward him, fully expecting, wanting, to die.

Then, as he bent his head to accept what would come, he saw his reflection in the water, white and shining. The rest of the story is mere coda. A happy ending, like all happy endings.

"Lady," the man says, so quietly it is almost a whisper. I turn to him. He is silent for a while, looking around as if he suspects someone might be spying on him—on us—as if we have a secret to keep. "Look. I want to show you something." He opens his jacket, and I see its fine lining. Someone paid a lot for this jacket once upon a time. Maybe the man himself did, in one of his earlier lives.

"Beautiful," I say. "They don't make linings like that anymore. Is it silk?"

"No, not *that*," he says. "Look closer. See?"

I lean toward him but can see nothing except a few scruffy feathers peeking from the inside pocket of the jacket. He lowers his voice even more, and I have to move closer to hear him. Yesterday, he tells me, as he was playing his guitar in front of the Met, some kids pointed to something on the sidewalk beneath a canopy of trees. A baby bird, they told him, had fallen from a tree. At first he didn't believe them. Kids always laugh at him. "They'll say anything to a person like me," he says. But as he got closer to the sidewalk, he saw that they were telling the truth.

I ask if he was afraid to touch it, because some people say that if you touch a baby bird, the mother will reject it once she catches your scent. He answers that no, he wasn't afraid—and, by the way, that's a myth about the mother—but he waited around a while anyway, just to be sure the mother wouldn't return.

The bird must not be a fledgling, ready to leave the nest; it must still be a nestling. A baby bird fallen from so high will certainly not last long. The man leans back on the bench and, as if sensing my thoughts, says, "So I thought, why not put her here?"

A winged shadow—a Canada goose, or maybe Pale Male himself—passes over us, but I don't look up. The pigeon is still positioned firmly on the man's shoulder, pivoting its head nervously, as if sensing danger. Baby, the birthday dog, drowses beneath the shopping cart, her chest rising and falling with each breath. The man slips his hand inside his jacket, over the silk-lined pocket. "I'm letting her go quietly," he whispers, "in a soft place." I imagine the warmth filling his hand, the urgent hammering of the bird's heart against his chest.

Su–Thrivingly

A FEW YEARS AGO, when I announced excitedly to one of my teenage nieces what Donald had given me for my fiftieth birthday, a look of panicky confusion crossed her face.

"A what?" she said, her blue eyes wide and unblinking.

I realized what she might be thinking. "Not an IUD," I said. "The *OED*. The *Oxford English Dictionary*."

"Oh," she said, visibly relieved. "That's nice."

Nice. The word came up a lot over the next few weeks, whenever someone asked me how my birthday went. "What did you get?"

"The *OED*. The complete set."

"Oh. That's nice."

I guess you're either someone who gets excited at the prospect of owning twenty gilt-stamped, deep cobalt blue buckram-covered volumes weighing in at approximately eight pounds per volume—that's eight pounds of words, multiplied by twenty, that's 160 pounds of words, at your hungry, grateful fingertips—or you're not.

Sublet lives on page thirty-six of Volume XVII (*Su–Thrivingly*), squeezed between *sublative* and *sub-lethal*, which gives you an idea of the neighborhood in which most sub-derivatives dwell. It's a big neighborhood, eighty-five pages wide and containing such notables as *subliminal* and *subconscious*, along with hundreds of subnotables: *subhuman*, *subfamily*, *subdwarf* (less luminous than dwarf stars), *subclimax* (don't ask, don't tell).

I always take special care with *Su-Thrivingly*, which, ever since that unfortunate encounter a few months ago, I've thought of as "Sue." I feel protective of Sue. She's the only volume with a visible wound: a quarter-inch rip on her blue spine, right beside the gilt-stamped "Second Edition." I blame the landlord's bicycle, which hangs from a giant hook near my desk, right in front of the stack of boxes I needed to get to that morning. No problem, I thought, I'll just squeeze between the back wheel and the boxes, just lift the wheel a little, nope, a little higher, a little higher, over that blasted hook, Geez it's heavy, but if I can just get my shoulder under it . . .

Had one of the office workers in the building across Fifty-Fifth Street happened to glance out the window at that very instant, he would have seen an upside-down bicycle and a smallish woman of indeterminate age flailing her arms, her mouth an Edvard Munch silent scream as the bicycle plummeted, toe clips spinning, handlebars coming to rest on a wall-mounted shelf filled with large blue books. From his vantage point, he couldn't have seen the aftermath: the woman sprawled across the parquet, rubbing her shoulder and whimpering softly. Not for the shoulder—it would heal—but for *Su-Thrivingly*, who had absorbed the blow for all the other volumes. Poor Sue, who must wear forever the history of that day, a gouge in her collectible cover.

Now stationed at my desk, I caress the wound on her spine. Just a nick. The nick of time. Nothing to cry over, for inside her sturdy buckram, the sub-children are still intact. The dreaded *Subpoena*. The maligned *Subhuman*.

Stoop-shouldered *Subservient*, backing her way out the door. *Submissive*, who's always known her place.

Turn another page, and the others begin to gather. *Subshrub*, who, though not as big as his shrub siblings, nevertheless stands his ground firmly. *Substantial*. *Subtle*. And *Subsistence*, wisest child of all, for how much do you really need, after all, to keep on keeping on?

Turns out, not so much. Not long ago, on April's first fine day, I was in line at the dry cleaner's. Correction: *on line*. I have to remember that's the way you say it up here. At the counter, an elderly couple was unloading a pile of heavy woolens, their winter lives destined for storage. The woman turned to me, shrugging apologetically. "Before we moved to the city," she said, "we had an attic."

I nodded, offering a look that said *I know, I know*.

She smiled and spread her arms, as if to embrace the whole city. "Now this is our attic." They counted out four coats, eight woolen scarves, three hats, and one fur wrap. As they turned toward the door, she slipped her arm into his, and together they walked out, in newly lightened bodies, into the spring air.

The Jury is Out, Reading

THE JURY ROOM IS so quiet I can hear Juror #1 swallow as she sips coffee and turns a page in her book. Jurors drink lots of coffee. We seldom speak. The first day of the trial we gabbed about the weather and complained about the long subway rides, the nonfunctioning bathrooms, the X-ray machines we must pass through when we enter the court-house. But since all that had brought us together is the trial, which we are not allowed to discuss, we soon retreated into our respective silences.

Now, mostly we read. And wait. We wait for the court-room to be cleared then refilled, for the lawyers and judge and witnesses to assemble and reassemble, for our lunch or-ders to be delivered by the bailiff, a congenial man with a thick Bronx accent, the open face of a schoolboy, and the chest of a heavyweight wrestler.

This is my fourth time serving on a trial, though my first time in New York City. Friends and students are amazed that I haven't caught on yet. There are dozens of ways to get out of it, they tell me: during the selection interviews, pre-tend to fall asleep, be sarcastic or disrespectful to the law-yers, act like you're high on something, make racist or sexist or ageist remarks. At times, I've imagined trying some of these tactics, but the truth is, as much as I detest most of the jury experience—they don't call it "serving" for nothing—I feel it's the least I can do. To play my small part in helping to grease the squeaky wheel of justice, to give something back to the city that's finally beginning to feel like home.

Besides, even if I tried to get out of jury duty, I'd probably get selected anyway. "It's your face," one friend told me. "You have no guile." This isn't true. I have as much guile as the next person; it just doesn't register on my face.

Juror #1 turns another page in her book, a best seller about biological weapons. "Looks like scary stuff," I whisper, the post-9/11 anthrax scares still raw in my mind. She's a criminal justice student, in her early twenties I guess, and she wears clingy tops and form-fitting jeans frayed fashionably at the hem. Beside her, Juror #3 studies a pamphlet with lettering too small for me to decipher. Across the table, Juror #5, a young attorney who just last week passed his bar exams, reads *Harry Potter*.

The jury room holds a simulated wood table, eight chairs (six for the jurors and two for the alternates) and a large round clock with a second hand that jumps. The scene has the feel of after-school suspension, or what I imagine after-school suspension to be. I wasn't a troublemaker in high school and I'm not one now, nor are any of my fellow jurors as far as I can tell. We follow the rules. We don't discuss the case, and when we leave for the day, we turn our yellow legal pads face down on the table. When it's time to assemble for our courtroom entrance, we line up and enter reverently, single file, to take our assigned places. I am Juror #2 and would not dream of taking the seat belonging to Juror #1. I confess that I occasionally sneak a peek at Juror #3's legal pad. The judge didn't expressly forbid us to read each other's notes, and it's hard not to since we're seated so close together and Juror

#3's handwriting is so large and loopy. Yesterday she jotted down something the prosecutor said about the length of the drugstore aisle. It didn't seem important at the time, but now I'm wondering if I should have written it down too.

I glance around the jury room, trying to read the faces without being noticed. Didn't some Shakespeare character say that juries might contain individuals more guilty than those on trial? Alternate #1 grips a paperback tightly in both hands—a legal thriller. Juror #6, a magazine editor, reads an Annie Proulx novel. Juror #4, a well-dressed blonde with an expensive haircut, reads a hardback edition of *The Corrections*. Is there a *functional* family anywhere, I wonder, and if so, would anyone want to read *their* story?

Directly across the table from me is Alternate #2, a powerfully built juvenile corrections officer who wears a gold medallion on a thick gold chain. He's reading the sports pages, which must not qualify as news or someone surely would have said something. Reading the news, the judge has warned us, is forbidden during the course of the trial, though I can't imagine that details about this trial—a trip-and-fall injury case against a big name drugstore—would be covered in the media. It's not a criminal case, after all.

Still, I'm staying away from newspapers. Instead, I've brought *The Merchant of Venice* to research a troubled poem I've been working on. Poetry, as William Carlos Williams wrote, isn't news. "Sorry," one of my students protested when I mentioned Williams's famous line, "but I just can't take seriously anything written by someone named Bill Bill." How little it takes to discount someone's testimony. That was years ago, and I still can't read Williams without thinking of the student's comment.

Actually, what Williams wrote was that it is difficult to

get the news from poems, "yet men die miserably every day /
for lack / of what is found there." I agree. If I didn't believe
poetry was newsworthy, I wouldn't have kept at it these past
thirty years. The draft I'm working on is about the mercy
seat, but it's not the seat described in the Old Testament,
the golden covering of the Ark of the Covenant where the
tables of the law were kept. And it's not the Johnny Cash
version about a death row inmate who takes his place on the
electric chair. The mercy seat I'm writing about is in Central
Park's Shakespeare Garden, an obscure collection of winding paths edged with stone and bordered solely with plants
and flowers mentioned in Shakespeare's work. I go there
whenever I need solace or consolation. I went on the morning of my fiftieth birthday, on the day I received the cancer
diagnosis, and on the first anniversary of the Trade Center
attacks. And I continue to go there on unremarkable days
when the crowded loneliness of the city becomes too much.

The mercy seat isn't its official name. I call it that because of the plaque on the back of the bench—"A Gift from
Sue and Gene Mercy." Mercy: a wonderful name to bear
throughout life; I'd choose it any day over Justice. Which
leads me to *The Merchant of Venice*, Portia's famous courtroom speech, which I've been reviewing while I wait with
the other jurors:

> The quality of mercy is not strain'd;
> It droppeth as the gentle rain from heaven
> Upon the place beneath.

Portia was pleading to Shylock for the life of someone she
knew, so of course she argued for mercy over justice. We

never cry out "Have justice upon me!" or upon those we love or represent. Justice we reserve for the other guy.

But who is the other guy in this case? The plaintiff, an elderly woman who alleges that while walking and talking with her daughter in the aisle of a drugstore, she tripped over boxes that should not have been there in the first place, and subsequently fell, injuring herself in the process? Or the defendant, the drugstore in the human incarnation of a night manager who admits to having placed the boxes there but who denies that his actions created conditions that could be judged dangerous?

We've been told to leave our sympathies outside the courtroom, a task more difficult than it sounds. Case in point: because I am a dictionary junkie, each time the judge reminds us to leave our sympathies outside the door, I can't help but imagine *sympathy*, like a many-petaled flower, growing from the Greek root for *suffering*. I am not to suffer with the plaintiff or the defendant. Nor can pity influence my decision. So, yesterday I stared stonily when the plaintiff's eyes filled with tears, and the eyes of her daughter. And when the attorney mentioned the plaintiff's age, I tried not to think that she was the same age as my mother.

But now, Portia is softening me up. I can almost see her standing before me in her lawyer's disguise:

Though justice be thy plea, consider this—
That, in the course of justice, none of us
Should see salvation.

Maybe it would be better, for justice's sake, to choose non-readers as jurors. Reading is all about sympathy. Passionate readers absorb books into their systems; some of us breathe in words like air. As a young woman, my sympathy for words led me to memorize dozens of poems, hoarding them like the root cellar potatoes my grandmother stored away for nourishment during lean, dark winters. Which came, of course, as they do in every life. One particularly desolate year, reciting those poems saved me from what I now understand was unspeakable despair. In great measure because of what I found there, I did not die miserably. More to the point, I did not die.

I've heard of jailhouse conversions, of people whose lives were turned upside down or right-side up by something they read: St. Augustine's *Confessions*, Plato's allegory of the cave, *The Autobiography of Malcolm X*. I read of a former Grand Wizard who had become a Klansman after reading hate literature and then turned away from the Klan after reading the Bible; of a Sing Sing convict so desperate for words that he had a long passage from *The Diary of Anne Frank* tattooed on his back. Through books, lives are changed, rearranged. Opinions are formed and reformed, behaviors altered. Will Juror #1 look at the world more soberly now that she's halfway through the book on biological weapons? She seems older than she did when the trial began, but that might be my imagination. Still, having lived vicariously for several days in a universe of plague, anthrax, and smallpox, how can she possibly emerge unscathed? Now that she's glimpsed the underworld of secrecy and plots, she may be less willing to believe a witness's testimony.

And what about the blonde juror who is just now surfacing from the final pages of *The Corrections*? Maybe she's thinking that the plaintiff's family is dysfunctional too, that the daughter, angrily testifying on her mother's behalf, was herself the negligent party. Shouldn't she have seen the boxes in time, pulled her mother out of harm's way? Parents and children: a minefield of possibilities, I'm thinking as I reconsider a line in my poem, a reference to Shylock's betrayal by his daughter.

Maybe I shouldn't be thinking about Shakespeare's Shylock, his sharpening the knife blade against his shoe, demanding his pound of flesh. Because Shylock makes me think of the prosecuting attorney, who I don't much like. Shylock brought an actual scale for measuring the flesh. The attorney in our courtroom invokes a metaphorical scale, asking us, the jurors, not only to decide that the woman has been mightily harmed, but also to weigh her pain and suffering in terms of dollars.

But I'm getting ahead of myself, ahead of the judicial process. We haven't yet heard all of the testimony, and we've been instructed to keep an open mind. The testimony is often boring, repetitive. It's difficult to remain active and three-dimensional, but as the judge keeps reminding us, it is our civic duty to bring all our instincts to bear. So each morning my eyes sweep the courtroom, focusing in on details. Sometimes I get carried away, noting things that have no bearing on the case, like the plastic statue of a crouching lion, its mouth open in a silent roar, which sits on the bailiff's desk. (Could it be that the bailiff is not as mild-mannered as he appears?)

Mostly, though, I stick to relevant points: the way the medical expert tilts her head when asked a question, the number of times the prosecuting attorney mispronounces his client's name, the pattern on the drugstore manager's tie. I squint to see if the plaintiff has recently gotten a professional manicure, a luxury I can rarely afford and which might suggest thriftless prodigality, even greed. The judge has asked us to apply the same kinds of tests we apply in our everyday life—our human, gut reactions—to what we hear and see in the courtroom. My gut tells me I don't believe the daughter. Or does she just remind me of someone—Shylock's daughter, perhaps, who comes off smelling like roses but is hardly blameless?

If this were a capital case, I would be more worried about my ability to judge fairly. Having entered the pages of Medea's story, how might I weigh in on the case of a mother accused of killing her children? Or, serving as a juror on a sexual abuse trial, should I come clean about my admiration for *Lolita*? And what of *Crime and Punishment*? If I were hearing the testimony of a student admitting to having committed a random murder, my memory of Raskolnikov's crimes might sway me, though in which direction—mercy or justice—I cannot say. I hope I would do what one of Shakespeare's characters advised: "Go to your bosom . . . Knock there, and ask your heart what it doth know." But I fear my heart would remain divided.

The bailiff enters the jury room, announcing that the trial will resume in the morning; we are free to leave for the day. Above the head of Alternate #1, the minute hand jumps, and she closes the courtroom potboiler with a satisfied sigh. She looks smug, as if she knows something we don't. Will she be able to mentally separate the fictional trial from the real one? It sure looks like her mind is made up: an open-and-shut case. Beside her, the young attorney reading *Harry Potter* seems mightily engaged in a battle with Lord Voldemort and the Death Eaters, a battle he could well carry into court tomorrow. And who could fault him? Who wouldn't choose dragons and house-elves, moors and lightning-bolt scars over hours of stagnant testimony? We're human beings, after all. It's been a long week, and we've listened hard, taken our civic responsibility seriously.

This time tomorrow, the lawyers will finish their closing arguments. After the two alternates are taken to a separate room, the remaining six of us will be sequestered. We'll vote, point for point, on each of ten questions, arguing politely about the definition of pain and suffering and calculating aloud the cost of each. Minute by minute, the large hand on the clock will jump, and by the end of the day justice will be served, and perhaps a little mercy too.

But for now we're zipping up our jackets and stuffing our books into our bags. The bailiff escorts us to the long, narrow corridor that leads to the elevator. When I turn to thank him, he smiles his boyish smile. I was right all along; there is no lion in him. We ride the elevator down to the lobby, where we wave goodbye and wish each other a good night's rest. Tomorrow we will meet here for the last time. One by one we will pass through the X-ray screeners. If the buzzer sounds, the officials will pat us down, checking for potentially dangerous items: guns, knives, razors. No one will search us for books.

Tomas the Shocker

ONE OF MY COLLEGE friends—an elaborately troubled girl whose long legs "I imagine go all the way up," an admiring man once told her—once moved from a lovely garden apartment into a furnished room above an ambulance garage, expressly for the purpose of being reminded, daily and nightly, of how close to the edge her life was teetering. I thought of her last month when I heard an NPR story about the man who calls himself "Tomas the Shocker." Tomas delivers electrical shocks to people in Mexico City bars: ten pesos per hit. "It's worth it," regulars say. Tomas can deliver up to 150 volts, but most people can't take more than seventy-eight. Surprisingly, some women can take more than some men. Some hold hands and let the charge run between them.

I admit that there have been times in our long marriage—Donald's and mine—when I would have taken any hit, paid any price, to feel that kind of charge again. I've felt that way about old friends too. For us, the old friends are an out-of-town couple loved for so long that we can remember the pattern beneath their newest upholstery, and the pattern before that one. I remember liking the old patterns better. People should leave a little bit of the original fabric showing, the way refurbished lobbies of historic hotels allow you a glimpse of the layers beneath.

Not long ago, we were at our friends' home for a weekend visit that feels now as if it happened to someone else. Maybe to you. Imagine sitting across the room on the newly upholstered sofa as your friends describe in ecstatic detail the young couple who'd visited a few weekends ago, sleeping in the guest room that until this moment you'd considered your own. As the friends speak, the spark in their eyes tells you that the house must have glittered from the light of the young couple, candlelight flaming, all the old stories made new. You listen and nod, a whiff of jealousy rising from your chest. It's rising from your husband, too; you can sense it, knowing him so long and well as you do. He's imagining it, too, how good it would feel to be once again the new couple, the guests romanced.

The moment passes, as such moments do, and you yawn from the cognac, slip off your shoes, pull over your feet an afghan you gave your friends one long-ago Christmas when you all sat up too late beside the glittering tree. It's been a long time since you sat up too late.

Tonight you will retire early to the guest room, where one dresser drawer still holds the weekend clothes your friends have stored for years now—your outdated jeans and soft pajamas, warm socks for the chill. You'd forgotten that drawer. How could you have forgotten it? Opening it now, your own history rises, your husband's too, and your history with your friends and theirs with you, and all of you still breathing.

In the morning you will meet your friends at the breakfast table wearing worn robes and tired faces, and you will sip the coffee your friends always serve dark and rich, sweetened with real cream, and you will lean back into the comfort of not needing to speak, thinking maybe this is what it comes to, and maybe this is enough.

Our Towns

ON THE PLAYBILL COVER, the minute hand of a pocket watch ticks its way toward the next hour: five o'clock. Cocktail hour, I'm thinking, though this thought says more about me than it does about the play. More likely, the playbill artist was indicating five a.m., a few minutes before dawn, a few minutes before the Stage Manager delivers his first lines and the sound technician cues the electronic offstage rooster.

This revival of *Our Town* marks Paul Newman's first return to Broadway in nearly forty years, and if that interval is any indication, this may be our last chance to see him onstage. Our history of theater going—Donald's and mine—is a history of missed last chances. We didn't know they were last chances at the time. Some were limited runs. Some were promising shows that suddenly, inexplicably closed. And some ran for so long that we took it for granted they would always be there, so why hurry to see them? The 9/11 attacks changed that for us. Though a night out on Broadway is an extravagance, we now try to see as many shows as we can afford.

I remove my wool gloves and slip my hand into Donald's. My hand in his is my way of reminding myself of our good fortune—to be alive in this city, to be together after all this time, after all that has passed between us. I am not by nature sentimental, so I need such reminders and must work hard not to feel embarrassed by them. As I must work hard, while I sit in the theater, not to feel embarrassed by what I know is about to be acted out: simple, homely sentiments. Ordinary people, ordinary days. The smell of heliotrope, the clink of milk bottles on the doorstep. Births and courtships and marriages and deaths.

A well-modulated male voice comes over the PA system announcing that the show is about to begin and would we please unwrap any candies in advance and turn off our cell phones and beepers. I glance around the theater: a sprinkling of young people, but the audience is mostly middle-aged and older. An elderly man in front of us struggles out of his overcoat. Beside him, a thin woman removes her hat, revealing a thick gray chignon from which a few hairpins are coming loose. The twenty-something woman to our right is asking her companions what the play is about, saying she only came because of Paul Newman. For me, watching Newman—in movies, on television—is a bittersweet experience. He looks like my father. The likeness is stunning: the same straight nose, the same blue eyes, and, in the past few years, the same thinning white hair. It took me decades to learn to love my father wholly, without reserve. In matters of the heart, I am a slow study.

The lights dim, playbills rustle. A plump woman on our left leans close to a young woman who might be her daughter. "I played Mrs. Gibbs," the older woman says. Community theater, I am thinking, or maybe college or high school.

"I'll bet half the people in the audience have been in it," I whisper to Donald.

He nods. Back at our apartment, in a box of mementos, is Donald's high school yearbook: Columbia, South Carolina,

1965, his junior year. The photo on page ninety-nine shows a teenage Donald made up, badly, to resemble a man about his age now. The caption reads, "After weeks of practicing to stay in character, the *Our Town* Stage Manager finds it hard to act his usual self." Someone has spray-painted his hair gray and drawn worry lines across his forehead. Or maybe the makeup person simply darkened the worry lines already in place; Donald inherited his mother's furrowed brow. By the time I met him, ten years past his debut as Stage Manager, his forehead was already intricately etched.

Deeper in the box of mementos is my yearbook: Santa Ana, California, 1967, my junior year. I played Rebecca Gibbs, George's slightly obnoxious little sister—chosen for the part, I imagine, because of my small stature. Or maybe for my smart mouth. I wanted to play Emily, but you take what you can get.

"Remember," our drama teacher said as he handed out our scripts, "there are no small parts, only small actors." Mr. Bush was always saying things like that. "Acting isn't about delivering lines," he would say, which made no sense to me. "It's about listening. Listen to the other characters. Respond to what they're saying." Rumor had it that Mr. Bush had gone to New York when he was young, and when he couldn't make it in the theater he came back to California and had been teaching ever since. Mr. Bush was short and squat, with a deep, commanding voice. Earlier that year, he had cast himself as Creon in the school production of *Antigone*. I thought it strange then—and now find it stranger still—that he should do this. Were there no high school boys who could play the part? Or did he consider this the role of a lifetime, in a lifetime that was running out?

At our first rehearsal, Mr. Bush suggested that all cast

members, no matter how minor (though he never called any of us minor) read the entire script and even compose biographies of our characters as a way of "inhabiting" them. But I was too busy counting my lines to listen to some old man's advice, even if he had once lived in New York.

I found consolation in my small part by reminding myself that, though my lines ended with act 1, I got to be on-stage for the wedding scene in act 2, which meant a costume change. True, I had to wear the same blue ribbon in my hair, but I got a different gingham dress. Gingham, according to Mr. Bush, was Rebecca's signature, one of the keys to her character. I argued with him, saying that Rebecca had aged three years since act 1, so shouldn't she wear something, well, something older? Character definition was the last thing on my mind; I just wanted to look pretty, like the character Emily Webb, who got to wear a white dress and veil. "She's the bride," Mr. Bush reminded me, as if I needed reminding. Like many high school girls of the time, I'd already planned my wedding, slicing photos of bridal gowns from magazines and pasting them into a scrapbook. All that was missing was the groom.

Whatever happened to that scrapbook? And to the girl who had kept it? At my first wedding, circa 1970, I stood before a minister wearing a gown and veil that my cousin had worn four years earlier. My father certainly would have sprung for a new dress; it was my idea to wear a borrowed one. What does that say about my character and the character of the marriage-to-be? It was my wedding, for godsake. Wasn't it worth the extravagance? I can't remember. It was all a blur, even as it was happening. Donald says it was the same for him. That same year, three thousand miles from California, he too was standing before an altar. It was a rushed affair, a bare-bones set, only the principals present: minister, parents, groom, pregnant bride. "A shotgun wedding," he jokes today, but no one was laughing then. I have asked to see pictures. He says there weren't any.

⸰⸰

But I'm getting ahead of myself, leaping to act 2, Love and Marriage, while act 1, Daily Life, is still in progress. When Paul Newman made his first appearance onstage, I had to look hard to find him. Later, when critics review his performance, they will mention the quiet way he "insinuated" himself onto the stage in semi-darkness, keeping his back to the audience as he delivered his opening lines, so as to short-circuit the applause that almost always greets a star's entrance onto the Broadway stage.

Newman's behavior seems fitting not only because he is a self-effacing actor but also because the Stage Manager isn't really the star of the show any more than God is the star of the Bible. I think of the Stage Manager not as a character but as an eye, a voice, a presence. Though housed in body—in this case the lean, wiry frame of a vibrant septuagenarian—the Stage Manager seems bodiless. Who were his parents? How long did he live in Grover's Corners? He keeps saying "our town," but we get no details about his connection to the place. I imagine that if we were to strip him bare—the concept of Stage Manager, I mean, not the human actor—his belly would be smooth as a stone. No umbilicus, no cord to tie him to the past or future, or to any particular father, mother, daughter, wife.

It must be a terrible burden to have been around forever, like God. To know in advance how each personal drama will unfold yet be unable, or unwilling, to influence the outcome. To stand by, hands crossed upon your chest, your pocket watch ticking, and observe it all being acted out, decade after decade, century after century. No wonder the Stage Manager keeps his distance. No wonder his delivery is so droll, his affect so affectless.

Still, beneath Thornton Wilder's lines a sadness lurks, a darkness. "My, isn't the moonlight terrible?" the young Emily asks near the end of act 1. Terrible as in awe-inspiring, beautiful? Or as in dreadful, terrifying? Everyone in town, it seems, notices the moon that night: Emily Webb and her next-door neighbor, George Gibbs, doing their homework at their respective windows; their mothers pausing on their walk home from choir practice; even the self-absorbed little Rebecca, who has announced early on in the play that what she loves most in the world is money. (I remember milking that line for all it was worth.) Rebecca climbs up to her brother's window because, she complains, the moon doesn't shine into hers. Perched beside her big brother, both of them staring out at the brightness, she has her moment.

"George," she asks, "is the moon shining on South America, Canada and half the whole world?"

Then, after being assured by her brother that it probably is, she realizes for a brief, terrifying moment her puny place in this huge, spinning globe, a realization that leads to her defining speech, which closes act 1.

⌘

Though I didn't save my script, I remembered my lines for many years. Donald says that he did too, which seems amazing considering the number and length of the Stage Manager's speeches. The pages of Donald's script are yellowed and mildewed, the torn cover secured with tape that has grown dark and brittle with age. He seems to have had trouble pronouncing particular words; *pneumonia* is underlined twice, and *genealogists* is broken into five distinct syllables. Certain speeches seem to have caused him trouble, such as the speech about marriage that the Stage Manager delivers in act 2:

"Do I believe in it? I don't know. I suppose I do. M marries N. Millions of them . . . Once in a thousand times it's interesting."

During the intermission between the first and second acts, while skimming the cast notes in the playbill, I notice that Newman has downplayed his acting credits, choosing instead to announce that he is married to "the best actress on the planet." A planet is a big place. Maybe Newman's marriage to Woodward is the one in a thousand Wilder is referring to. I have no right to assume this, but it is hard not to. We watch, we wonder, we put two and two together.

Or one and one together to make one—another way to think of marriage, or so the Army chaplain said, over and over, three or four times a weekend, to the couples standing before him at the altar. Married less than a year, I was the vocalist for a military chapel, performing at weddings to help pay the household bills while my husband was away at boot camp. Already my own wedding was a blur. At twenty-one, just five years after playing George Gibbs's little sister, I felt like an old woman. Or a young woman playing the part of an old woman. Meanwhile, three thousand miles away in South Carolina, furrow-browed Donald was also finding it hard to act his usual self. He had been drafted into the Army and was playing the part of a soldier, while his wife of five months was in a hospital hundreds of miles from him, delivering a ten-pound son.

Both marriages lasted three years. I prefer *lasted* to *ended*, though the truth is, both marriages ended badly, mine even more badly than Donald's. Still, when friends and family urged me to toss the wedding photographs, I found that I couldn't. Maybe I needed proof that it had not been a dream. In one photo, a blue-eyed, dark-haired man is leading me down the aisle. He looks so young—was my father ever that young? There must have been so much he wanted to say.

∽∞∾

Emily and George's wedding represents an aesthetic turning point in the play. Up until now, the audience has heard only what the characters reveal through conversation or physical gesture. Now for the first time, we overhear what is in their hearts. Emily's mother rails against the cruelty of sending girls out into marriage and laments her own "blind as a bat" experience. George wants to know why everybody is pushing him so—he just wants "to be a fella." Emily confesses that she has never felt so alone in all her life.

Though the actors deliver these lines while onstage with other actors, the audience senses that no one onstage can hear the characters' deepest thoughts. It seems right that Emily doesn't hear her mother's frantic outpouring, and that her mother doesn't hear Emily's lonely cry. If we all voiced our deepest selves to one another, what would become of us? I imagine first a vibration, then a distant hum that approaches slowly, indistinctly, as each of our voices finds its pitch, its timbre, culminating in one unearthly, communal roar—all the world's love, hate, terror, joy, and fear gathering momentum until our ancestors, sensing the vibration, rise from their graves and join in.

Wilder would not approve of my dramatic detour. According to the Stage Manager, there are practical reasons for keeping our mouths shut. If brides and grooms knew what they were getting into, life as we know it would disappear. "Nature," the Stage Manager reminds us, has been "pushing and contriving for some time now." Our silence may well be a part of that contrivance. For the good of the species, we best keep ourselves to ourselves. As George and Emily's parents did. As our parents did, allowing their actions to speak louder than words. In this way, Mother Gibbs (who will die within a few years of her son's wedding, though no one knows this yet) takes her husband's hand and leads him to the porch to smell the heliotrope under the light of the terrible moon. And the morning of their son's wedding, wrenching back tears, she sets the breakfast table and makes French toast, which, if we can surmise from her husband's delighted reaction, is one of his favorite dishes.

George and Emily were lucky to have parents like this, doubly lucky if they witnessed such gestures of affection and constancy. The most minor scene between loving parents can carry a child through. Early on, I caught glimpses: my father kissing the back of my mother's neck, the flushed glow on my mother's face when he returned from an overseas mission. Donald, too, recalls childhood moments like these. Despite the difficulties that must have existed in our parents' marriages—the whispered soliloquies, the asides, the strained dialogues delivered sotto voce over the heads of the dinner table audience—neither of us ever doubted our parents' devotion to each other or to us.

I now know this to be an extraordinary gift they gave us. Ordinary people achieving something extraordinary. Without such a history, would Donald and I have weathered our own dark years? There was no child to bind us. Unless you count Donald's son, who, eight years after making his first appearance as a strapping baby, showed up at our doorstep wearing a man's worried forehead. "You're not my mother," he repeated to me, belligerently, sadly, month after month, year after year. You're right, I would think, never voicing my thoughts aloud. I'm barely a wife.

∽∞∾

The New Age maxim "There are no extra people" doesn't apply in the theater. Someone is always waiting in the wings, ready to take over if you can't go on. Donald doesn't remember having an understudy, but he must have, because when he contracted laryngitis before opening night, someone stepped in at the last minute, someone whose name is not listed in the yearbook. Little consolation that Donald got to perform on the second night—with a microphone, he recalls, though he can't be sure. What he *is* sure of, what he can't stop remembering all these years later, isn't what happened but precisely what didn't: the lines he didn't get to say on opening night, lines he had labored to make his own that now belonged to someone else.

So it goes. You rehearse and rehearse, plot and scheme. Then life steps in and does away with all your plans.

But the understudies are ready. They too have been working for weeks, months, years, mouthing lines from their offstage perches. Hoping, fearing that one night they will get their turn. If they are patient, they probably will.

Principal actors get sick, they sprain an ankle, lose their voices, their heart. Marriages end. You acquire a second husband and his son. You take a deep breath, step into your mother's worn shoes, mouth the words someone wrote for her years ago—and for her mother, and her mother before that, and her mother before that. "I know, honey, I know," my mother would croon over and over to whatever ache I was suffering. I was only one of her six children, seven if you count the baby girl buried before I was born, but in that moment I was her only. Her words weren't what soothed me. It was her rhythm, her body, the way she leaned into my ache as if it were her own. As if this were the first time she had ever appeared in such a scene.

⁘

Wilder stipulated an intermission after act 2, but in the Newman production act 2 runs into act 3 with only a momentary pause and a minor set change. A blink of the pin-spot, and nine years have passed. Chairs that had been filled with wedding guests are now filled with the dead—rows of characters with placid, still demeanors. The unnamed church lady is there, and Mrs. Gibbs, and Wally, and a half dozen others, many identified in the script only with monikers such as "1st Dead Man" or "2nd Dead Woman."

Chances are you remember that Emily joins the dead ones, a heroine of sorts, having given her life in childbirth. What you might not remember is that Emily still wears her wedding dress. The Emily in my high school production wore the same white dress I had coveted all during act 2 and never stopped coveting, even when it became Emily's death shroud. After all, Emily never actually looks dead, not even when she decides to rewind the tape of her life and haunt her family's kitchen on the morning of her twelfth birthday.

At this point, I am thinking that the Stage Manager should take Emily by the shoulders and give her newly dead face a gentle slap. Wake her up to what he's about to say. Instead, he keeps his distance, delivering his warning in the same low-key, casual tone he has used throughout the play: "You not only live it; but you watch yourself living it." Yet despite this warning, and against the advice of the other dead ones, Emily insists on a return visit to the world she believes she once inhabited.

And who could blame her? Who wouldn't want a chance at that? Once, during a bleak time—our thirteenth married year, Donald lost for months to an understudy playing my role—I would have exchanged all my futures for one day's return to an earlier happiness. The closest I got was a visit to my parents' home, where I quietly cried myself to sleep each night. Days were spent mostly in the car, my father at the wheel. One day, crossing the farmlands of his childhood, we were recalling aloud the many cross-country trips our family had made. "I'd like to make that trip west one more time," he said.

"We can still do it," I said, my mind, desperate to survive the present moment, churning with memories: the '57 Chevy wagon, the Scotch plaid cooler Mother packed with sandwiches and treats, all of us kids stuffed into the back seat and Way Back, taking turns playing shotgun to Dad's all-night marathons—me uncapping his coffee thermos, pouring a cupful and handing it to him while the rest of the family slept and cacti and stars whirled past. "We can chart the old Route 66," I said. "Stop at the same places. The Wagon Wheel Motel in Albuquerque, that Stuckey's in Barstow where we got the free peanut brittle—"

My father lifted one hand from the steering wheel, stopping me in mid-sentence. "You don't understand," he said quietly, a sad smile crossing his lips. "I want it to be *then, now.*"

Then, now. Of course, I thought. Impossible.

I carried his response back to my silent bed and then, days later, back to my silent home. Even after Donald returned, it would be months before I again thought of the home as *ours.*

Then, now. What Emily imagines she can have but can't, knowing, as she now knows, how the future of this moment will play itself out. Too much knowledge is dangerous. What if you knew the whole play in advance and discovered, for instance, that the life you were playing would be finished before the opening of act 3? Would you, like Mrs. Gibbs, go ahead and make the French toast anyway?

And what of the survivors, those who must plod through to the curtain call long after losing the heart to carry on? Like Mrs. Webb, who loses both her children—Emily to childbirth and Wally to a burst appendix—before the play's final blackout. Hard enough to bear these griefs after the fact. If she knew in advance what was coming, would not her grief be doubly hard?

Maybe not. Maybe if we knew how long each of our moments would last in the big scheme of things, we would be better able to weigh them as they were happening. Case in point: the presence of Wally Webb at the breakfast table, the boy no one really notices because he has only one line. Wally's presence weighs more than it seems to. Though only eleven, he is already long past middle age, if we take into account his actual lifetime. (He will be dead from that burst appendix before act 3 opens.) So, let your middle-aged boy read his geography book in peace, Mrs. Webb! Stop scolding for a moment, hold that bowl of steaming oatmeal in mid-air a few more seconds, and really look at him. Listen to his one line: "Oh Ma! By ten o'clock I got to know all about Canada." A splendid line, when you really listen to it. And the boy has a point. Canada is a big place; there is so much to learn.

⌀∞⌀

Had I heeded Mr. Bush's advice to study the whole play, to read between the lines, I might have had more sympathy for Rebecca's character, more insight into what he had called her *motivation*, her *heart*. Many years would pass before I discovered Donald's script of *Our Town* and, for the first time, read the play in its entirety. How could I have missed so much? Wilder's story stretches far, wide, and deep. As far as stars and distant galaxies, as wide as centuries, as deep as the layers of Pleistocene granite buried deep below Grover's Corners. Even a character as minor as Rebecca Gibbs has depth, width, and breadth if you look closely enough. Her existence stretches beyond her meager lines, beyond even her onstage presence. Apparently she leaves town somewhere between act 2 and act 3 to elope with an insurance salesman and live in Canton, Ohio. Soon afterwards, her mother visits and promptly dies of pneumonia, the disease that the teenage Donald had such trouble pronouncing.

Mother Gibbs's death must have come as a great shock to Rebecca. Did she have time to sit at her mother's bedside and offer comfort? Donald's own mother went quickly. We had thought she had weathered the worst—the most recent prognosis had been good, and the chemo seemed to be working. Then one September evening just weeks after our twenty-one-year-old son (when had I started calling him ours?) had left to reunite with his flesh-and-blood mother, we got the news. Donald's mother had taken a turn for the worse, and more suddenly than anyone had expected, her lungs had given out.

"How does it feel?" I ask friends whose parents have died, eager for a clue. "How do you move on, how do you bear it?" And again, "How does it feel?" Time after time they answer, "It's not how you think it will be." You can plan and plan, my friends tell me, and then suddenly they are gone and you are left feeling—well, feeling nothing at first. Or everything at first and then nothing. One friend had no words for her sorrow. Another could not stop talking. One friend felt heavier, weighted down. Another had never felt lighter, freer, which made him feel guilty until he gave up trying to understand any of it.

Donald's reaction to his mother's death was stoic, matter-of-fact. Or so it seemed at the time. "How do you feel?" I would ask, night after night, month after month, lying beside him in his silence. Then one night, out of the blue, moonless dark that filled our room: a sound. I turned to Donald but he was gone, replaced by a full-grown orphan with Donald's face but shrunken to some earlier version of himself. And what was this wetness on his pillow? Tears, so many months later?

I stretched my arm across the pillow and leaned close, my mouth against his ear. "I know," I began shyly, hesitantly. And then stronger, more confidently, growing into the part, "I know, honey. I know. I know."

A train whistles stage right. A clock strikes. "Eleven o'clock in Grover's Corners," Paul Newman says, winding his watch as he finishes his last speech. "Tomorrow's going to be another day. You get a good rest too. Good night." Wait, I want to say as he exits downstage left. I'm not ready yet, I'm still in act 2: "You know how it is," Newman had said, crossing down center to make his point. "You're twenty-one or twenty-two and you make some decisions; then whisssh! you're seventy; you've been a lawyer for fifty years, and that white-haired lady by your side has eaten over fifty thousand meals with you . . ." Fifty thousand meals, I am thinking, trying to do the math, and I am seeing Newman and Woodward at their breakfast table, and Donald's parents at theirs, and my parents at theirs—fifty thousand meals!—and Donald and me at ours, then whisssh, our eight-year-old boy is thirty-one, living out West and raising some other man's son, and just think, all my teachers are dead though their words still live in my head: lean in close, read between the lines, listen, listen as if it were the first time you have ever heard them. Play each scene as if it were new.

The lights come back on, brighter than before, and we are tossed into the present moment: this theater in the center of our living, grieving town, my hand slipping out of Donald's so that we can both clap, loudly, steadily, because it is curtain call, time to give something back. Time for everyone to take a bow—even Dead Man #1 and Lady in the Box and that amorphous clump appearing from the wings, the People of the Town. A long line forms across the stage and our applause thickens and broadens until we are all one pair of hands clapping as the line breaks apart and Newman appears in the center. He seems smaller than he did earlier, more ordinary, his white hair so soft and fine that I want to reach out and touch it. As he lowers his head for the bow, I see for the first time a patch of pink scalp. He bows deeply, reverently, and calmly walks off the stage.

Ginkgo Song

ABOVE THE TUNNEL AND across the park in this city that never sleeps, everyone, it seems, does. Sometimes in late morning, I walk to my favorite bench in Sheep Meadow and wait for the sleepers to wake. Now, scanning the green lawn before me, I see a man and woman stretched out together, face down, shoeless, the *New York Times* carefully arranged like a pallet beneath them. One of the woman's pale hands rests lightly atop the man's T-shirted back—a tender, domestic gesture, one I often commit on Donald while he is asleep.

Near the couple, near enough to be in an adjoining bedroom if the sky were ceiling and these trees were walls, the muscled torso of a man curls around a ginkgo trunk as if he were growing out of it. Two orange crutches and a guitar are carefully placed beside him, and, beside the guitar, two artificial legs tapering to stumps below the knee joints. The way we take off our shoes to sleep, he has taken off these legs.

Watching the sleeping man, I keep thinking of the man on the subway, the tall, beautiful, copper-colored man I once stumbled awkwardly into when the train took its squealing, violent turn right before South Ferry. "So sorry," I said. "Forgive me."

The man nodded but never looked down at me. He remained upright, strongly positioned, his face like a carving on some ancient coin. When he spoke, each word was perfectly calibrated, clear, calm as a still lake: "Let Calgon be Calgon."

I blinked and forced myself to look away from his beauty. Another crazy, I figured. Lord, they're everywhere: The woman preaching at me through a restroom door, holding the Holy Bible above the stall with huge Moses hands. The pregnant girl screeching like a wild bird in the lobby of Grand Central, then screaming to everyone in hearing distance—that would be all of Manhattan—that she needed money for insurance because her husband was "emotionally unavailable."

I grabbed for the subway strap and recovered my balance, looking again at the beautiful man. He was still beautiful, still calm, and, I suddenly realized, absolutely sane. My mother used to sprinkle Calgon into the laundry to soften our clothes and into the bathtub to soften her dirt-crusted, callus-footed children. *Let Calgon be Calgon*, his private mantra generously shared with me, a Zen koan that made so much sense it didn't need to make any. *Calgon*. A long-ago, used-up word, rescued from the tossed-out bin of my child-hood. Yes, I thought, let Calgon be Calgon. Let it soften the hearts of all us calloused children, grown now, up and away from the lives our parents jump-started all those years ago.

Suddenly I am very sleepy, the best kind of sleepy. I want to curl up like the legless man before me, surrounded by bird squawk and squirrel chatter, the way I used to curl up in the middle of the grownups' talk—my uncle shuffling the cards, my aunt stalled in the middle of a story with no point except its telling, my mother's conspiratorial laughter. Pretending sleep, willing my arm to flop dramatically onto the sofa so that they would let me stay right there, part of the scene but even more so, lone sleeper in the midst of all that song. I would like to fall asleep right now, on this bench, waking to the snap of the plastic legs socketing the man back together, and, in a few minutes, the strum of his guitar.

Biographical Note

REBECCA MCCLANAHAN, author of ten books, has received two Pushcart Prizes, the Glasgow Award in nonfiction, the J. Howard and Barbara M. J. Wood Prize from *Poetry* magazine, and four fellowships from the New York Foundation for the Arts and the North Carolina Arts Council. Her work has appeared in *Best American Essays*, *Best American Poetry*, the *Georgia Review*, the *Kenyon Review*, the *Sun*, and in anthologies published by Doubleday, Simon & Schuster, Norton, Houghton Mifflin Harcourt, Bedford/St. Martin's, and numerous others. She teaches in the MFA programs of Queens University and Rainier Writing Workshop and lives with her husband, video producer Donald Devet, in Charlotte, North Carolina.